extraor

leadership

extraordinary
leadership

CREATING STRATEGIES FOR CHANGE

PETER J REED

RECOMMENDED BY
INSTITUTE OF DIRECTORS

KOGAN
PAGE

This book has been endorsed by the Institute of Directors.

The endorsement is given to selected Kogan Page books which the IoD recognises as being of specific interest to its members and providing them with up-to-date, informative and practical resources for creating business success. Kogan Page books endorsed by the IoD represent the most authoritative guidance available on a wide range of subjects including management, finance, marketing, training and HR.

The views expressed in this book are those of the author and are not necessarily the same as those of the Institue of Directors.

First published in Great Britain and the United States by Kogan Page Limited in 2001
Reprinted in 2002
First published in paperback in 2003

120 Pentonville Road
London N1 9JN
UK

22883 Quicksilver Drive
Sterling VA 20166-2012
USA

© Peter J Reed 2001

British Library Cataloguing in Publication Data

A CIP record for this book is available from the British Library.

ISBN 0 7494 4043 0 (pbk)
      0 7494 3512 7 (hbk)

Typeset by JS Typesetting Ltd, Wellingborough, Northants
Printed and bound in Great Britain by Biddles Ltd, Guildford and King's Lynn
www.biddles.co.uk

For my father, Owen Reed

1920–1991

Contents

Acknowledgements

The ideas that form the basis of the discussion and advice in this book have taken over 30 years to develop. Many of them are not original and are, in fact, a synopsis of what I believe to be the best theoretical material available. To qualify as 'best', for me the ideas have to be practical and the models have to be capable of operational application with proven results. Consequently all of the ideas included are those that I have personally applied and found to be very valuable – usually in the course of advising clients around the globe in the most complex of major change programmes.

I am most grateful to the following colleagues, friends and organizations for their generous support and for the use of their ideas and materials:

Andrew Cooper of Mindworks for the use of the Mindworks Approach and for his helpful comments and contributions for Chapter 6 (www.mindwks.com).

Steve Bratt and BQC Performance Management Ltd for their advice and for use of BQC materials supporting the EFQM Excellence Model in Chapter 8 (www.bqc-network.com).

Dave Richards and Derek Medhurst of D&D Excellence for their advice on Chapters 7 and 8 and for the use of their diagram showing the alignment of the scorecard and Excellence Model (www.ddexcellence.com).

The European Foundation for Quality Management (EFQM) for the use of the Excellence Model, which is a registered trademark of EFQM (1999).

The Fellows of Harvard University and Harvard University Business School Press for quotations from *The Harvard Business Review* and for the excerpt in Chapter 5 about the eight-stage process for leading major change from John Kotter's book, *Leading Change*.

Robert Bacal and his publishers McGraw-Hill for the excerpt from the Briefcase Book, *A Handbook of Performance Management* in Chapter 11.

Sanjay Saxena for his advice on e-business and e-commerce and for the story about 'getting the big stones in first'.

Renaissance Consulting (USA) for the use of material from their Renaissance White Paper, 'The Balanced Scorecard – An overview' in Chapter 7 (www.rens.com).

In particular I would like to thank Martin Treadway for his extraordinary professionalism and for working so rapidly on the cover design, and my editor Emily Steele and Kogan Page for their belief in the concept, for their patience in always having to maintain contact via difficult communications media, and for their sound advice. As ever, I am eternally grateful to all my clients and associates – both at home and around the world – for all that they have taught me both directly and through the provision of opportunities to turn good ideas into good practice.

Finally, I must thank my family and especially my wife Bridget for their belief, patience, interest, encouragement, support and inspiration.

Introduction

The genius of a good leader is to leave behind a situation which common sense, without the grace of genius, can deal with successfully.

Walter Lippman

The use of the word 'leadership' and the concept of its exercise normally apply to situations where a team of people or an organization has a mission or a task to achieve, and that someone, or perhaps some group, is 'in charge' of this process, and has authority and accountability for both the process and the results. It is, and always has been, about responsibility for converting a vision for a future state of being into reality: usually a reality that is presumed to be preferable to the current one. This is achieved through strategic thinking as a vehicle for strategic planning, and through developing and coordinating the skills and strengths of individual team members, while maintaining cohesion of the team as a whole, so that strategy is the means to effective action. It is about championing the definition and clarification of a vision and inspiring others not only to 'sign up' to it, but to commit themselves enthusiastically to sharing responsibility for the process of implementing strategies to achieve it. Often it involves leading and coordinating the process of major organizational change through considerable resistance and in turbulent operating environments. This is never easy.

In fact it involves what some have called the 'new work' of leadership – new adaptive and generative work which is more complex and not as objectively linear in its task orientation as the traditional perception that most people still hold of the role. One task of leadership is to understand complexity and reduce it, as Walter Lippman eloquently says, to common sense.

Much has been written recently about 'learning organizations' and some commentators now feel that leadership in the 21st century should be more about teaching and coaching to share lessons learnt through the development of teachable points of view, than about strategies, methodologies and tools. I believe that, as usual when new concepts become fashionable, there is always a danger of 'throwing the baby out with the bath water'. For many capable and potentially effective leaders there is a need both to understand strategy development thoroughly, and to find methodologies and models to help them get their insights across to others in a compelling way.

It has been said that every leader has to sell two fundamental things: solutions and positive feelings. If, however, leaders always deliver all the solutions themselves, old paradigms (if they exist), and resistance to change (which nearly always exists), may be merely reinforced, and unhealthy dependencies created. By the same token, if things conspire (as they usually do) to make the achievement of desired results even more difficult than anticipated, the subsequent post-mortem 'blame storming' will undoubtedly find an easy scapegoat. It may be more appropriate in most cases to suggest that leaders have to sell the 'need' for solutions and the sense of urgency for others to find innovative ways to achieve them. This will usually involve team members taking responsibility themselves for the adaptive ideas and work inputs that they will be required to generate. Encouraging and empowering them to do so is one of the new, and in my experience uncommon – and therefore extraordinary – leadership responsibilities and skills.

Leadership is also about managing performance on the one hand, and managing uncertainty on the other. It was probably ever thus, and no doubt it seems to every generation that they have to manage more uncertainty than their predecessors. In recent years we have, however, learnt much about how performance can indeed be 'managed' more effectively, and doing this provides 'solutions' in the form of improved business results and customer satisfaction. Uncertainty is by definition more difficult to manage and consequently unsettling. Yet it is more than ever a fact of life and a corollary of change – a 'given' in the fast-moving and often unstable economic climate in which business and other organizational leaders must produce these results. Perhaps its ultimate manifestation to date has been the phenomenal growth of the Internet, and with it the exponential multiplication of opportunities for e-business and access to the global marketplace. In 1948 the CEO of IBM predicted that the world market could probably tolerate four computers. Ten years ago there were just 50 sites on the World Wide Web. Today there are more than 10 million. Who could have had any sense of certainty about such a development, or of its impact?

To manage both performance and uncertainty successfully requires that leaders recognize and role model the essential differences between management and leadership. The skill is to 'hold' the dynamic tension which exists between the tendency for effective and efficient management of performance to lead to complacency (the seductive impression that one can somehow control measurable variables in an unstable world), and the discomfort that most people feel with too much concentration on (or even attention to) uncertainty, with all its normally negative and disquieting connotations. Managing organizational discomfort is undoubtedly a leadership responsibility as well as a leadership competency. Introducing greater efficiency into performance improvement initiatives with an aspiration to optimize performance outputs continuously towards total quality is too, but it can be seen as 'ordinary management' which will not, on its own, produce extraordinary results. One can, in fact, achieve significant, measurable and quantifiable improvements in many individual processes, but the overall organizational learning may have limited sustainability. What is needed is a leader's ability to see the whole picture as a 'system' and recognize the interdependencies. Some processes can be, and need to be re-engineered, but often this will have an impact on the smooth working of the larger system. You have to apply systems thinking and teach others to do this in order to frame continuous organizational learning. The need to develop these competencies will be a recurrent theme of this book. Helping managers and staff to cope with (or even thrive on) the challenge of continuously learning to learn, while recognizing that the apparent stability that their undoubtedly worthwhile 'ordinary management' produces is illusory, is definitely more extraordinary. It is necessary in extraordinary times, and it requires extraordinary leadership.

Overcoming the natural human tendency to be risk-averse, or to shun innovative habits that may sometimes produce short-term pain, is also something that extraordinary leaders have to help their organizations (and this means their people) to do. Leaders need to learn these skills and they need to help their organizations – that is to say their people – to learn continuously in order to stay abreast of, or even anticipate change as, a way of life. This is true now perhaps more than at any time in the past. Indeed, as Modahl (2000) suggests is the case for the majority of businesses, it is probably 'now or never' if they are to manage change in order to win the battle for the Internet customer. Speed and a permanent, all-pervading sense of urgency are now essential to remain competitive or to retain competitive advantage.

The following chapters take the reader logically and pragmatically through the process of understanding the dynamics and the mechanics of this approach to strategic systems thinking for major change. They provide practical advice on how to implement continuous performance improvement and how, at the same time, to stay 'in balance' if not entirely 'in control' when everything seems far from certainty, or when even the agreement of others, who may not possess this ability to hold the overall systems view in mind, is itself an uncertain commodity.

Systems do not, of course, operate in a vacuum. They are established for a more or less clear purpose, and they operate in the context of an external environment where social, legal, environmental, political and technological factors all impact upon the workings of the system and the ability of its managers (and particularly leaders) to read the signs of these impacts, to learn from them, and to respond with interventions to improve overall systemic performance as a result. Specialist knowledge of any part of the system will sensitize those in possession of it to specific and often quite esoteric ways in which they may be able to seek out and identify areas for improvement or re-engineering of system 'components' or processes. This competence together with the necessary degree of empowerment and authority to implement such improvements can breed laudable concern for and commitment to quality management. Only the ability to take the overview and see the whole system, and thus be able to determine the effects of interventions on other parts of the system and its interdependencies, can provide senior management with an awareness of 'total' quality. Only the ability to communicate a vision for this in understandable terms can sell the benefits of it to the majority of employees and assist the empowerment process in any enterprise or organization. The former ability (ie practical demonstration and role modelling of commitment to continuous improvement) is a required management competency; the latter is one required of leadership.

The issue of the extent to which it is possible to plan strategically for a desirable future state of affairs raises many interesting questions. There is no question that strategy often emerges – and perhaps with hindsight we can often see that this frequently happens despite, rather than as a result of, the most careful and rigorous planning. Nevertheless, my own experience on the ground, often in extremely turbulent operating environments, tells me that in general planning is better than no planning. Good planning should after all be an iterative process not just an occasional ritual conducted in isolation from reality, and an important part of the cyclical process that should inform it is the feedback from an analysis of the success or failure of the implementation of plans to date. The doyen of management consultants, Peter Drucker once wrote: 'Plans are worthless, but planning is invaluable.'

The value lies, of course, principally in the learning to be gained from the exercise and the 'learning curve' is in reality a learning cycle with both positive and negative feedback loops. Dealing with the learning from the latter takes initiative and innovation and a prepared-ness to try new and perhaps challenging strategies to arrive at the desired future state. It may be possible, in a well-developed organization with a high performance team, for this learning to be accomplished quickly and continuously, and the more this happens the more teams can become effectively self-managing for the purposes of delivering planned outputs. I have never yet met a situation, however, where what others have called 'self-managing teams' will do anything other than stay competently within their comfort zones. To encourage them out of and beyond this state, and to enable or empower them to achieve extraordinary results, requires some out of the ordinary stimulus. I believe that this can only be provided by the right kind of inspirational and extraordinary leadership. For example, a well-integrated team may be able, through experience and knowledge of one another's skills and aptitudes, to clarify the common goals and interdependencies between team members. Only a good team leader can leverage the team's synergy to get results beyond agreed targets. This may even involve the management of potentially creative tensions inherent in the group process to forge innovative solutions.

This leverage of team synergy is particularly valuable during the strategic and operational planning process. It stems from any good leader's ability to create a compelling and inspirational picture of the future, regardless of how difficult the present reality may be, how limited the resources appear to be, or how many impediments exist in the form of inappropriate existing structures or paradigms.

What an effective planning process does above all else, in addition to identifying the strategic and perhaps visionary results areas and organizational objectives, is to break these down into 'bite-sized' pieces to which individual managers or team members can relate. Indeed they will often be prepared (or even keen) to be held accountable once they can see the logical connections between their inputs and the overall planned organizational output or purpose. It most certainly isn't all analysis, breaking down or re-engineering, however. It frequently and increasingly now involves synthesis of interdependent activities for the overall strengthening of the organizational system. The plan becomes, in effect, a holistic organizational health and fitness regime.

What a truly effective leader does (perhaps above all else) is to see connections, trends and patterns in all of this (and the operating environment) that are not at the time obvious to others, and to make a vocation of developing this capability in colleagues. The logical connections to which I have just alluded often appear at first sight to be 'binary'. That is to say the logic of their connection is essentially vertical and is derived from (or underpinned by) the hierarchy of organizational or perhaps project planning objectives. At every level however, from the most strategic to the 'grass-roots' operational, the required outputs and any inputs to achieve them have interdependencies and effects on one another. Decisions will have what Mant (1997) calls 'ternary' or three-dimensional effects. Attempts to re-engineer processes that may perhaps be seen as less than wholly efficient when viewed in isolation may result in adverse effects on other parts of the 'system'. Closing down railway branch lines because they are not profitable may cripple the larger national network that they were supposed to feed, as British Railways found to its cost in the 1960s. Not only was the larger transport system almost fatally damaged, but the impact on the wider social 'system' was also significant and damaging. Effective leadership minimizes the risk of, and the incidence of such mistakes, but as this ability to take the overview, perhaps while personally engaged in the thick of the day-to-day corporate action is seemingly not a common competency, we must conclude that it is one important feature of what I have called 'extraordinary leadership'.

Bennis (1984) refers to research he did in the early 1980s. He says:

> Leaders are people who do the right thing; managers are people who do things right. Both roles are crucial, and they differ profoundly. I often observe people in top positions doing the wrong things well. Given my definition, one of the key problems facing American organizations (and probably those in much of the industrialized world) is that they are underled and overmanaged. They do not pay enough attention to doing

the right thing, while they pay too much attention to doing things right. Part of the fault lies with our schools of management; we teach people how to be good technicians and good staff people, but we don't train people for leadership.

My own experience in a number of developing countries tells me that this is not just a malaise particular to 'much of the industrialized world'. It also applies to developing countries, many of which have over-bureaucratized institutions – particularly in their public sectors, and particularly if these have been developed through socialist command economies, soviet-style systems, or even, it has to be said, the influence of civil servants of the British Empire. Look no further than the Indian Civil Service! In such circumstances 'the right thing' tends to be perceived as short-termist despite the ideology often theoretically having a longer-term vision in mind, and such perceptions are frequently transposed to serve the self-interest of those in the ruling elite. 'Doing things right' tends to mean maintaining the status quo of the existing system or of protocols that have been established over a long period to serve such interests. Any new 'right thing' will usually require new ways of 'doing things right' and this is both difficult and threatening. Managers, according to Harvard's Professor Abraham Zalesnik (1977), 'view themselves as conservators and regulators of an existing order that they personally identify with and from which they gain rewards'. Understanding this, and more to the point being prepared to challenge the status quo, takes courage that is undoubtedly out of the ordinary.

It is a sad fact that the greater good (which is usually a longer-term vision) often takes a back seat in the public sector in developing countries. Consequently it is relatively easy for politicians and public servants to pander to the public's and the international community aid donors' natural impatience to see and feel the benefits of change in immediately tangible ways that are unfortunately often at the expense of sustainability.

Zalesnik is right. Leaders must be prepared to promote a new view that constantly challenges all existing structures and they must do this within a context and underpinning framework of values and high principles. In doing so they may create even greater turbulence than that which exists in the operating environment they are helping their organization to address, but ultimately they cannot fail. This will require continuous facilitation of the individual and corporate learning process through which all other processes are challenged, adapted and improved and through which creative solutions and frequently extra-ordinary results are attained.

Noel Tichy, a long-time observer of General Electric and its CEO Jack Welch (*Time* Magazine's 'CEO of the 20th Century'), is convinced that the single most significant aspect of Welch that makes him an extraordinary leader is his commitment to developing leaders at all levels of the organization, and the amount of time and energy he is prepared to spend in teaching and developing other leaders. Quoted in a recent issue of the Indian business monthly, *Business Today*, he points out that despite having to run the world's largest company (judged by market capitalization), 60 per cent of Jack Welch's calendar is spent on leadership initiatives and that his major focus is on building leadership. Somehow he finds the time to do this so it's not about time, it's about priorities. Furthermore Tichy points out that although learning is necessary, it is not enough. He prefers the concept of the 'teaching organization' where, as in the US Navy's Special Operations units, when people learn something they believe is useful, they immediately teach it to all their team members.

This is what I have tried to do in this book. I believe that instinctively we all try to distil and synthesize the best of what we see and hear when it strikes a chord with our own 'field' experience, and we blend this essence with the practical learning and pragmatic competence that we have gained from this experience. I have gained much of the latter from over 20 years of helping others to deal with change and if I have learnt one thing in the course of gaining this experience it is that the common denominator everywhere is the need for principled and strategic leadership. *Ordinary management* is no longer enough. *Extraordinary leadership* is required and if this book can help in a small way to make extraordinary leadership less extraordinary, it will have served its purpose.

In summary I have tried to combine two things. The first is an exploration of what I believe to be current best thinking about leadership as it is now so clearly needed in many, if not most organizations. The second is a very practical summary of a series of models that constitute what I believe to be best practice. The models not only neatly and graphically explain how to develop systems thinking and how to lead the improvement of vital business processes, they act together as a practical toolkit to enable leaders to plan, coordinate and monitor the effectiveness of the application of these concepts in the workplace.

They are not original and I do not claim the credit for inventing any of them. Each, in its way, can offer extraordinary insights. In combination, and when used in sequence as I suggest, they will, I promise you, enable you to enable others and your organization as a whole, to learn to produce extraordinary results.

Part I

Context and challenge

1

The nature of leaders and leadership

Leadership is a combination of strategy and character. If you must be without one, be without the strategy.

General H Norman Schwarzkopf

PERCEPTIONS AND EXPECTATIONS

Are 'extraordinary' leaders born or can they be made? This is a new version of an old conundrum and the original argument has been so well rehearsed that it is easy to shy away from revisiting it for fear of being considered unimaginative, repetitive or perhaps seen as deliberately controversial or politically incorrect. There are, of course, numerous examples of famous leaders who were never trained for the role and who nevertheless somehow developed the competencies required to excel in it. I would dare to guess that the great majority of those who have been recognized as extraordinary would admit to, or even claim some pride in the fact that they learnt most of what they knew from experience and from those whom they were credited with leading. Furthermore, I venture to suggest that we now require a new and different form of extraordinariness. Being able to declare leadership extraordinary with hindsight is too reactionary and at best this would only be useful for our purpose if by studying its nature one was then able to 'bottle' its essence. Nobody has managed yet to do this although there have been many attempts to define or describe it. Taffinder (1995) seems to indicate that possession of a set of competencies that can manage these various dilemmas could be part, at least, of the formula when he says:

> *No one can understand leadership without recognizing that it is, at one and the same time, elusive but momentous, passionate but coldly single minded, a matter for patience but sudden opportunity, and a force to be grasped by ambitious individuals but nurtured by others. It is a capacity that flourishes in circumstances that may be hopeless, to achieve ends that may be triumphant or forlorn. In a sense it matters little which, for it is the great struggle for victory that is the ordinary habit of leadership.*

Is it perverse, then, that business schools in all developed countries appear to be convinced (and wish to convince potential customers) that the subject matter at least can be learnt? The reality is that, as I mentioned when quoting Warren Bennis in the Introduction, schools of management often tend to teach people to be good technicians and good staff people. They usually do not train people for leadership although some do claim to venture where others fear to tread in this regard. Is this clever sleight of hand to persuade people that knowledge and competence are one and the same, or indeed that management and leadership are? Is it perhaps opportunism born of universities' belated recognition that good money is to be made from programmes that claim to offer real business benefits, and that this is acceptable because it has now become a respectable discipline for the award of higher degrees? Has the pure and doubtless worthwhile academic study of historical events and behaviour patterns (in the world of commerce and business, just as in politics or military history) somehow provided more than subject matter; more than a body of data describing what effective leaders do? Has it really produced the answers necessary to design competency training programmes offering fail-safe operational guidelines to equip anyone for the role in any circumstances, or does the application of theory to practice always require a specific context?

What is certain is that while not everyone can be the chief executive of a multi-billion pound (or dollar) corporation, just as not everyone can aspire to be an Olympic athlete, with coaching and practice we can learn to be a lot better than we are at present. Leadership potential exists in many more people than ever get the chance to develop or show it. While business schools can and should see this as a challenge and a 'market', they should also take the longer view that over perhaps a generation, they can play a role in producing potential leaders who in turn can ensure that there will be an organizational ethos and atmosphere in their businesses that are able to nurture initiative and leadership potential.

EXTRAORDINARY CHALLENGES

Does real leadership perhaps require an unusual or particularly challenging set of circumstances that are 'out of the ordinary'; and can we conclude that all leaders worthy of the title are therefore 'extraordinary' because they can really only apply their knowledge and skills effectively in extraordinary situations? Perhaps the practice of effective management becomes leadership by default in such situations. Are we persuaded that the times in which we now live are themselves more extraordinary than ever before, and do we perhaps now have enough data, evidence and experience of training potential leaders and enhancing the skills of existing ones to be able to articulate sound practical advice on the subject and apply it to succession planning?

According to Taffinder one might conclude that none of this really matters because just as to travel is said to be more rewarding than to arrive, the 'struggle for victory is the ordinary habit of leadership'. What I believe distinguishes extraordinary leadership from this ordinary habit, is the capacity it has to achieve extraordinary 'victories' (to use Taffinder's word) in a proactive, planned and systematic way. As we shall see repeatedly throughout this book, proactivity, planning and systems thinking are essential elements of the special brand of leadership that is likely to be effective in major change initiatives or projects. The ability constantly to learn from the feedback provided by the system is perhaps the most important of all.

In justification of this book I have, of course, to say that in my opinion the answer to most of the questions that I have posed, and specifically to the last one about the possibility of training people for the role, must be 'yes'. Whether or not others could justifiably have said the same thing in the past, we certainly do live in extraordinary times with extraordinary challenges that require extraordinary leadership competencies, many of which can be developed. The caveat must be that knowledge is only a component of competence, and competence only comes into its own in an ethical context. Possession of all the theoretical knowledge in the world will not necessarily mean that effective (or for that matter ethical or principled) decisions will be made, or that effective action will result. To take a simple down to earth example: one might know all there is to know in theory about the correct way to discipline or dismiss a member of staff who consistently underperforms. Emotionally one might not even like the individual concerned, but when the chips are down, will you do it or 'duck' it? Tough decisions require 'guts', in business as much as on the battlefield. In both cases it is not just the development of strategy but what you do with it that counts. As Chris Argyris has often reminded us, espoused theory should be (but is rarely) congruent with theory in use.

It may be useful to consider the extent to which developments in society generally, information technology, and rapidly changing business operating environments in particular, have produced changes in our attitudes to leadership and leaders, and the demands we make of them. The effect of these environmental factors on the actual work of leaders will be considered in the next chapter and later. For now, let us consider some conventional perceptions.

TRAINING FOR THE EXTRAORDINARY – THE MILITARY PERSPECTIVE

The military have always recognized that leaders can, in fact, be trained or developed, although they have also tended throughout history to believe that 'trainability' depended somehow on a rather narrow view of aptitude and confidence. This, it was felt, was probably in-born more as a factor of presumed good genetic breeding than of any other scientifically or psychologically based analysis. If an aristocratic family consistently produced generations of sons who grew up expecting automatically to become military officers who had leadership thrust upon them, it was no doubt easy to believe that somehow it was 'in the genes' and that family connections were as important as other criteria or acquired characteristics in any selection process. Furthermore 'leadership' was assumed to be a quality that could from time to time be demonstrated by 'other ranks' in exceptional operational circumstances, but was required and assumed to be an innate characteristic in officers.

This view still existed in the British Army until very recently and cadets at The Royal Military Academy, Sandhurst, were (and perhaps still are) appraised on an indeterminate attribute called 'OQ' or officer quality. Its apparent possession was probably more a product of attitude (which to be charitable one could call self-confidence) than of learning or applied necessary skills, and in the view of some cynics its importance as an indicator has never been completely replaced by the more measurable criteria of true meritocracy. Somehow, however, we can all relate to the meaning of this phrase – 'officer quality' – which really refers to an ability born of self-confidence to inspire confidence in others. Is attitude an important component of aptitude or ability in this context? It may well be, if the latter is in the main a perception of third party observers, and the former an undoubted factor in the creation of such perceptions.

An ex-naval officer colleague of mine informs me that a question on naval officers' performance appraisal forms was (and perhaps still is): 'Would you be happy to be at sea with this man?' I am also reminded of the telling (but no doubt apocryphal) quotation from an army cavalry subaltern's confidential report that stated, 'I would hesitate to breed from this officer.' Although both of these sentences imply that very subjective and unquantifiable criteria must be used in the required judgements and conclusions, and although the quotations are amusing, somehow we all know what was meant, and we can all relate to the underlying implications. Leadership, like beauty it seems, is hard to define, but you know it when you see it.

In his book _On the Psychology of Military Incompetence_, Dixon (1979) famously catalogued the apparent failings of selection, training and strategy, and their impact on politics and society. If he were to write a sequel today I am sure that there would be just as many examples of this incompetence from the years since he first wrote it, as those in the history on which he originally commented.

Ordinary management and extraordinary leadership

An unfortunate corollary of the often completely illogical or apparently perverse 'career planning' that has traditionally been a sequel to initial selection and training in the military is that it has never really allowed for late developers. In wartime or on the battlefield rather the opposite is true, and bright youngsters may find themselves summarily and rapidly promoted to positions of great authority in which they may be lucky or clever enough to shine. In peacetime neither the opportunities nor the challenges have tended to exist in the military for individuals to demonstrate real leadership skills or qualities that are in any way extraordinary. In fact for the most part the military have recognized that much of what goes on from day to day in peacetime requires what they now recognize as management skills and what I have referred to above as 'ordinary management' processes. One of the reasons, however, that the quality of leadership at all ranks and levels in the British Army is, I believe, so high, is that the UK has been engaged more or less continuously in small wars and counter-insurgency operations around the globe since World War II. There have always been plenty of opportunities, therefore, in active service operational conditions, for enough soldiers at all levels of seniority to gain real (and for peacetime extraordinary) leadership experience and pass this on through training, and the continuous improvement of processes and equipment.

This is just as well, because the ability to identify organizational development opportunities or challenges in the form of what both private and public sector organizations might now call 'areas for improvement' was hardly encouraged in junior ranks. The ability to be constructively critical and take the overview, was for a very long time actively discouraged, especially in junior officers. They may have been selected in part for the ability to demonstrate initiative to a selection board, but woe betide them if they dared to demonstrate too much of it subsequently, or question the status quo – at least until they were seen to have the authority of a senior officer's rank and position to justify them to do so. The culture and the paradigm discouraged it.

I should admit at this point that these are easily scored points and that I do have a considerable respect and fondness for the military. I was born into a 'military family' and served for nine years as a professional Army officer after graduating from two years of study at the above-mentioned Royal Military Academy. I do therefore have some knowledge and experience of the general context, and of the specific, very different, and by definition extraordinary context of Special Forces, where for the best of reasons true meritocracy has always been much more apparent and important, and where extraordinary leadership is routinely required and demonstrated at all levels (ie ranks). The words 'special' and 'extraordinary' are probably, in fact, synonymous in this context. I will return to the conclusions that perhaps we can draw, and the lessons that business and other organizational leaders may be able to learn from this, later in the book.

ATTITUDE, APTITUDE AND LIFELONG LEARNING

A number of writers have noted in recent years that effective leaders (often those responsible for programmes of major corporate or organizational change) frequently emerge as late developers through the consistent application (perhaps subconscious or unintentional) of lifelong learning habits. It appears that this is often despite apparent lack of early success in the conventional education system, or barriers erected against their progress and their recognition of the need for change by vested interests in bureaucracies or large corporations. The ability consciously to discipline one's lifelong learning, or perhaps the need instinctively to keep as abreast as possible of change and its challenges, seems to be partly a result of balanced and stable psychological development that is free from damaging influences. Encouragement of broadband learning and empowerment for one's own personal development by caring parents, relatives and teachers are probably of incalculable value in this context.

Stability or constancy, in terms of both temperament and values, in an impressionable child's family environment seems to be an important contributory factor to later stable and functional (as opposed to dysfunctional) behaviour patterns. One can reasonably conclude that they are prerequisites for sound leadership ability. The connections are probably as logical and valid as those that psychologists make more frequently with regard to unstable or infamous leaders who throughout history can be shown to have often suffered damaging experiences in their formative years. Perhaps the most recent notorious example of one such who let his demons loose on others is ex-President Slobodan Milosovic of Serbia.

Certain individuals seem to get better and better at thriving on change and uncertainty – possibly as a result of the conditioning they have received through having to adapt to challenging and turbulent (but not psychologically damaging) careers or personal lives. Others fear change, and most are uncomfortable with the uncertainty it creates. The aptitude for learning seems to be enhanced by a facility to accept challenges and not be averse to some risk in so doing.

Clearly the psychological personality traits and styles of behaviour that exemplify this capability are well researched and able to be tested in well-documented ways. Those whom we tend to classify as leaders normally assume or inherit the title or description (and with it the 'mantle' with attendant expectations) as a result of their appointment to a position, the responsibilities of which require the management of people and resources to achieve tangible results. It is the balance of normality and uncertainty in the operating environment, the difficulty of the challenge, and the degree of risk that determine the degree to which the person in this position of responsibility may have to demonstrate what we would regard as true leadership skills, as opposed simply to the competencies necessary for the management of the processes and the human resources involved.

Major change initiatives are by definition 'projects' that generate the need to track and measure success in implementation. At the same time they tend to generate discomfort and fear of the unknown. To lead others in the implementation of such 'projects', leaders have to role model the ability to manage both performance and uncertainty at the same time. By being seen to do so they can also provide reassurance to those who are by nature less comfortable with this dynamic, but who must learn to find it stimulating rather than threatening. Helping a 'traditional' and perhaps successful business to cope with or even thrive on the challenge of e-commerce is a perfect example of this competence in action.

Fast fish and slow fish

It is often the speed of the required strategy development in this context that scares people and rightly so. Big fish do not necessarily eat small fish; fast fish eat slow fish! The speed that is required means that the learning curve is typically much steeper than it may have been for other new developments or ventures in the past. A report by Forrester Research in the United States reminds us that it took radio 50 years to become fully established with universal market acceptance. By comparison it took television only 20 years, and the Internet 5 years!

Not only has the slope of the learning curve become steeper: the height of it has also increased in as much as the technologies to be understood and managed are so much more complex, in design, in construction and in use. Fortunately the technology has brought with it the benefit that it is no longer necessary to know everything about a subject as long as you know where to find the information, and this is usually available on the World Wide Web by courtesy of this very technology.

Nevertheless the introduction of entirely new ways of doing business and their integration with the existing and conventional ways is bound to cause conflict. Implementing adaptive or generative work that challenges existing structures, attitudes and paradigms always generates conflict. Extraordinary leaders have to be able to depersonalize and externalize such conflicts. They must distinguish 'self' from 'role' by focusing attention on the real issues and by giving the conflict back to its rightful owners. This usually means those who must actually do the work.

Frogs and bicycles

In addition, using Alistair Mant's (1997) analogy, they have to be able to tell whether an organization is a 'bicycle' which can be dismantled, cleaned and re-engineered, or whether (as is almost always the case), it is really a 'frog' – in other words a living system.

Living systems normally have symbiotic relationships with others, and re-engineering or surgical treatment (even of parts which may appear to be 'bike-ish') may result in dangerous if not fatal consequences for them, and possibly for the bigger (eco)system of which they are a part! Just because new technology is at the root of the new ways of doing business does not mean that adapting processes, or generating new ones to incorporate it, should be a purely mechanical exercise.

Covey (1992) agrees that organizations are essentially organic and not mechanical. He also refers to the need to understand what he calls 'the mechanical versus the agricultural paradigm'. He points out that desired results in organizations are not achieved through engineering by mechanics or the replacement of non-working parts, but by nurturing over time – as it were by a gardener who knows how to create the correct conditions to maximize growth.

THE BASIS OF LEADERSHIP COMPETENCE

What we have just done here is to list a number of the skills or competencies that seem to set aside successful leaders. A lot of good work has been done in recent years in an attempt to define and frame such leadership competencies, and to determine whether they are, in fact, generic and applicable, for example to both public and private sector organizations. All of the models imply, if not explain, that competence is always dependent on, or perhaps a factor of the underlying context or operating environment.

Bennis (1984) states that it is important to place his survey findings, concerning the areas of leadership competence shared by 90 leaders, in context and to review them in the context of the moods and events in the United States (specifically 1960s–1980s decline and malaise) just before and during his research. After several years of observation and conversation he defined four competencies that he found to be evident to some extent in every member of his survey group of 60 corporate and 30 public sector chief executives. These were what he called:

- management of attention;

- management of meaning;

- management of trust; and

- management of self.

Bennis goes on to say that the collective effect of these competencies is empowerment of others, and specifically this is most evident in four themes:

- people feel significant;

- learning and competence matter;

- people are part of a community; and

- work is exciting.

Even a few years later, and admittedly with the benefit of even more hindsight, it seems now that most of this is surely self-evident. Did it really take a survey of 90 top leaders to tell us these home truths? Well, perhaps it did – and certainly at the time. It may seem like common sense now but as we all know, the trouble with good sense is that it is often not common enough; not then and not now! What seems to be far more interesting than these perhaps predictable statements describing the ethos in well-led organizations, is how leaders develop the traits and the styles and patterns of behaviour necessary to encourage the growth of this ethos, and how they balance the priorities for doing so at any given (possibly turbulent) time. Can we find out how they did this and teach others the tricks?

Furthermore, are the tricks that prove useful in one extraordinary situation applicable to others which are perhaps equally extraordinary but in a different way? They may be if the perceived required competencies are as generic as Bennis suggests. When doing this we need to distinguish between the development of leadership skills and competencies per se, and the overarching competency or capacity for their effective application – for example, to the development and nurturing of effective teams. Perhaps as Frances Hesselbein, President and CEO of the Peter F Drucker Foundation, says: 'Leadership is a matter of how to be, not how to do.' The eternal truth of these generic competencies is perhaps best understood when one attempts to define the differences between, or perhaps the common denominators, of what we mean by 'how to be' and 'how to do'. We may then be able to relate these to what may be the equally generic or fundamental processes of the leadership of major change projects or programmes. I will take a more in-depth look at the field of leadership competencies, competency frameworks and the influence of the competency movement in Chapter 13.

Perceptions of course always depend to an extent on where one is coming from. When talking about the key competency for 'the management of attention', Bennis describes how a young cellist, when asked about a great conductor responded: 'I'll tell you why he's so great: he doesn't waste our time.' This is interesting because it underlines the fact that such an insight requires that the respondent knows whether his or her time is being wasted or not. This in turn implies knowing the value of that time, and the concept of value has both monetary and intellectual dimensions. Both are ultimately constrained by the power to utilize them to good effect and then to indicate recognition of worth; a power that is usually in the hands of someone else. If this 'someone else' is not role modelling integrity for the longer term, how can one pursue one's conviction that one's time is too valuable to waste? Convincing people that they should pursue such a conviction of self-worth, when none of the desirable motivators, or even what Herzberg referred to as the basic 'hygiene factors' are in place, is part of the work of leadership – particularly in situations of severe budgetary constraint.

Power and influence

How hard this work proves to be is inversely proportional to the legitimate power of a leader and as Covey (1992) points out:

> *The hallmark of legitimate power is sustained proactive influence. Power is sustained because it is not dependent on whether or not something desirable or undesirable happens to the follower. To be proactive is to continually make choices based on deeply held values. . . Legitimate power occurs when the cause or purpose or goal is believed in as deeply by the followers as by the leaders.*

It is always relatively easy to lean on positional power or the authority of rank or status – particularly in cultures where there is traditional respect for rank and status for its own sake, or where power-distance between managers and subordinates is significant enough to deter at least overt disagreement or non-compliance. What is often hard (perhaps even extraordinary) is the capacity to remain true to deeply held values when under pressure or in the middle of a crisis. This requires what we often call 'true character', and its application often over a sustained period of time in order to build the sort of trust in relationships which cannot be fabricated ad hoc, and which does not emanate from formal duty alone. We are reminded again of Hesselbein's idea that perhaps leadership is a way of being as opposed to a way of doing things; and of Schwarzkopf's that character is ultimately more important even than strategy.

Compasses and maps

This 'way of being' exemplifies a habit of finding one's way through such crises by instinct and values. This process is perhaps akin to navigating more by compass than by map. One has to have belief in a true sense of direction rather than blind faith in a map that may have errors of detail or anachronisms built into it. I am indebted once again to Stephen Covey (1992) for several compelling reasons why a compass (ie a creed of ethically sound natural principles) is so much better than a map in today's business world:

▪ The compass orients people to the coordinates and indicates a course or direction even in forests, deserts, seas, and open, unsettled terrain.

▋ As the territory changes, the map becomes obsolete; in times of rapid change, a map may be dated and inaccurate by the time it's printed.

▋ Inaccurate maps are sources of great frustration for people who are trying to find their way or navigate territory.

▋ Many executives are pioneering, managing in uncharted waters or wilderness, and no existing map accurately describes the territory.

▋ To get anywhere very fast, we need refined processes and clear channels of production and distribution (freeways), and to find or create freeways in the wilderness, we need a compass.

▋ The map provides a description, but the compass provides more vision and direction.

▋ An accurate map is a good management tool, but a compass is a leadership and an empowerment tool.

Over-reliance on maps is rather like reliance on outdated mental models or paradigms that are no longer appropriate. Sometimes it may be very difficult to determine whether apparent resistance to what may well be recognized theoretically as necessary change (for example for the modernization of an organization or even a whole society or state apparatus) is rooted merely in an organizational paradigm which can and should be shifted, or in a much deeper and more intransigent societal or even national culture which may be fundamentally at odds with espoused theories of economic or public service development. To aspire to gain the commitment of society as a whole to the need for fundamental change is, of course, the mission of politicians. Those who achieve it undoubtedly require extraordinary skills of influence and persuasion, and in a democracy, just as effectively as in a boardroom, the majority will sooner or later pronounce its verdict on whether they consider the influence to have been, on balance, beneficial.

Such problems of the context in which leaders have to practise their art, their influence, or their skills often touch on the turbulence of operating environments and this is the subject of the next chapter.

2

Situations and operating environments

Why does every generation have to think that it lives in the period with the greatest turbulence?

Henry Mintzberg

'PLUS CA CHANGE!'

We suggested in Chapter 1 that many organizations and businesses could be forgiven for thinking that the constant and dramatic changes that they have to face in their operating environments seem to be unprecedented in their scale, their impact and the difficulties they create for effective strategic and operational planning. In fact it is a perennial complaint, and prompts Mintzberg (1994) to ask the above question.

The idea that we live in extraordinary times, and that as a result we must constantly re-engineer existing processes, gives rise to anxiety and an unfortunate tendency to ignore much of the good in what has gone before. It also fuels an unhealthy trade in consultancy of what I would call the 'orthopaedic surgical' variety, when holistic counselling or something more akin to a 'health and fitness regime' might be more appropriate. True cynics might even go so far as to say that a conspiracy has built up around this trade, affecting both private and public sectors, and especially in developing countries where the international donor community insists on paying for millions of dollars worth of such surgical re-engineering to be imposed by consultants on systems which become weary of the treatment. If anything, the 'beneficiary' organizations sometimes get sicker, thus precipitating predictable conclusions that managing change is, of course, notoriously difficult, and recommendations that more of the same 'treatment' is therefore necessary, literally ad nauseam.

In their thought-provoking book, Binney and Williams (1997) suggest that what they call 'living systems thinking' leads one to think that:

> _much of the 'change' which organizations are undergoing is self-inflicted: the result of managers desperate to force change through instead of working with the natural capacity of people and organizations to develop._

Trying to 'force change through' can, of course, be a mistaken strategy that often fails to take into account (let alone respect) the nature of the resistance that such initiatives can generate. It may, however, be the result of a leader's recognition (or the consensus of what Professor John Kotter (1999) of Harvard calls a 'guiding coalition') that the pressing need for a sense of urgency to pursue the espoused vision for the future requires this sort of approach – the end justifying the means. The implication is that if you don't push through the desirable changes that you need to get away from a current reality that is not in line with your vision for the future, you will inevitably become a victim of change anyway, but you will not be in control, and the changes thrust upon you may be to your detriment. I will return later to the 'top-down' versus 'bottom-up' argument about the most effective way to 'manage' change.

THE NEED FOR A SENSE OF DIRECTION

For now let us consider the issue of how we arrive at perceptions concerning the need for change. The concept of change management has indeed become such a fashionable one over the last 10 years that there is always a danger that management teams can fall into the type of 'group-think' that endorses the need for change for its own sake. The perceived desirability of being proactive, as opposed to reacting to threats in the operating environment, can lead one to forget that by standing in a stream one can determine its speed and direction and use this to one's advantage without necessarily aspiring to attempt the difficult task of altering its course.

Anyone who walks regularly in the mountains or hills will know that mountain paths have usually been established over generations, in some cases by animals that presumably have an instinct for these things. Although they do not always appear to follow what appears visually to be the most direct route, or the shortest one, they invariably get there safely in the end, and there are usually very good reasons why they follow the topography as they do. Although we may use them to arrive at a certain specific target point, their logic is often more one of their leading (albeit with many twists and turns) in the right direction. A true sense of direction (as it were from a compass) enabled those who first established them to pioneer their progress. The route thus established then became, over time, the basis of a 'map' for others to follow.

WHERE TO START WITH STRATEGY FORMULATION

There is a considerable body of argument about whether current reality (which is after all tangible and for which there can be no excuse for inaccurate analysis) is a sounder base on which to build strategy than a visionary picture of a future that we cannot even see, let alone guarantee. Binney and Williams appear to think that, on balance, it is. They state:

> *Starting with current reality is the foundation stone of an uncommon view of the way people in organizations change. Paradoxically the energy for change comes from becoming more aware of where the organization is now. . . Leaders in change work effectively with their own view of direction which they allow to be informed and modified by the emerging clarity of what is really possible. In some organizations, once people are really engaged and excited the leader's initial goal or vision can seem unambitious!*

I would agree with their view that the idea that there is no time to plan, or that there is little point in it because of the crazy pace of change (an idea that seems to have become fashionable through the writings of such eminent 'gurus' as Tom Peters and others) is certainly flawed and probably dangerous. I would also agree that even visions that are enshrined in longer-term strategic plans can, and should, be brought up to date iteratively in line with emerging 'current' reality. But the word 'more' in the phrase 'becoming more aware of where the organization is now' implies a deduced comparison with some other state (where we need to be perhaps), or at least the need for a systematic framework or model to help us analyse and enhance our current state of awareness with a view eventually to providing better-quality comparisons.

Reverting to the map and compass analogy we can see that in the case of the compass, it is not simply necessary to have the direction of true North as a guide. The instrument's deduction of where this may be is based on where it is at the time. The direction is a meaningless concept without reference to a starting point, so perhaps it is not really an issue of which of the current reality or the envisioned future state is the more important, but rather one of recognizing the need for a proper, and as far as possible an accurate appreciation of both.

Analytical tools

There are many models that can facilitate analysis of these two states and any 'gap' that may exist between them. Some, such as the well-known strengths, weaknesses, opportunities, threats, or SWOT analysis, imply comparisons and can therefore address the competitive dimension and aid strategic planning for commercially competitive advantage.

Others such as the SLEPT analysis consider the social, legal, economic, political, and technological factors inherent in the operating environment in which an organization finds itself. Such an analysis can be used to throw light on the direction an organization may need to take, and point to appropriate strategies for getting there, provided that there is some reasonably sound basis for predicting how these factors themselves are likely (individually and in concert) to affect the overall operating environment, and thus the organization's fitness for survival in it.

Another analytical tool, and one that has gained considerable currency and respect in the last few years since its original introduction by Kaplan and Norton in a _Harvard Business Review_ article in 1992, is the balanced scorecard. Its reputation as a powerful tool to help generate and embed systems thinking is well deserved, and it now forms the basis for a number of benchmarking methodologies for the planning, monitoring and evaluation of continuous improvement towards total quality.

Surprisingly, to my mind, its usefulness as a model for analysis of the totality of both the current reality and a desired or envisioned future state, thus defining the 'gap' by a number of dimensions or parameters, has not been widely appreciated. Nor has its use as a tool for strategy development that is congruent with a vision or even an aid to defining the vision. When it is used in this way it can make strategic plans less subject to the vagaries of emergent operating conditions – at least as far as this is ever possible. Where this has been attempted it has more often than not been in the public sector. I offer a more detailed description of the use and benefits of balanced scorecards in Chapter 7.

In the UK's Public Sector Benchmarking Project, for example, the use of the Business Excellence Model – now called the European Foundation for Quality Management's Excellence Model – has been refined over a period of seven years. This is a balanced scorecard model that encourages management teams to consider how to generate continuous improvement, and benchmark the extent of this, in performance results and service delivery standards. The analysis is done by considering nine key criteria (five enablers and four results areas) that encompass all aspects of the business or organization under the following headings:

Enablers	*Results*
leadership	key performance results
policy and strategy	customer results (satisfaction)
processes	people results (employee satisfaction)
partnerships and resources	society results (impact on society)
people (human resource) management	

Self-assessment by executive teams using this model can generate a baseline score by means of an internationally recognized scoring system. Even more worthwhile than the baseline score, however, is the usual realization when employing this model, that the insights gained are simply too important and fundamental to be omitted from the strategic planning process. This planning process is frequently conducted in a soundly 'classical' way by considering 'where we are now' – the current reality, before trying to envision a nebulous desired future state (where do we want to be?), and somehow from this to determine strategic objectives and priorities for action. Many will relate to the crisis of confidence that the uncertainties of this process can engender. A detailed description of how the Excellence Model can enrich the strategic thinking of this planning process, in order to shape your strategy to arrive at the future you want with more confidence, can be found later in this book in Chapter 8. A detailed guide to producing a strategic plan follows in Chapter 11.

Putting the future first – vision versus current reality

What I have found to be particularly helpful is to use the nine criteria of the model to frame the management team's 'picture of the future' before doing a similar analysis for the current reality. Why do it this way round? The answer is that if the current reality is depressing, if the current structures are 'given', and without doubt an impediment to progress, but it has never occurred to anyone that it may be possible to look beyond them, and if all around is 'gloom and doom' on the resources or financial front, people find it extremely difficult to be 'bullish' – or even what an outsider might consider to be realistic – about a picture of the future. In Chapter 6, I describe a systems thinking process to facilitate strategic planning that adopts this approach.

It may be as unwise as it is unrealistic for organizations in such situations to compare themselves in a competitive sense with 'best-in-class' organizations or world-class performance. Such comparisons could, if not handled sensitively, be seen as irrelevant and can be even more depressing than the reality of the immediate economic surroundings. There is, however, a sound body of data and information about what good practice looks and feels like and there is nothing wrong with learning from the best. Management competencies in the context of key process identification and improvement are, for example, well documented and for the most part essentially generic, as are good human resource management practices. Even the realization that no mechanisms currently exist to map customer or employee satisfaction levels, points to the need for this to be seen as an area for improvement – and probably a priority, if actions are to be taken that can remedy the situation and produce benchmarked improvements in future.

Such an exercise, using a balanced scorecard methodology to provide a very detailed analysis of what the future could look like, has the result of unblocking prejudices about the impossibility, or fixed nature, or structures of the current situation or operating environment. Typically between 100 and 150 areas for improvement (AFIs) will emerge from the 'gap analysis' and even more surprisingly, most of them would probably not have been considered in a 'traditional' analysis of the existing situation, mandate, mission, functions or structure of the organization. The scope and definition of key results areas and strategic objectives can be immeasurably improved through this process, and the most difficult job then becomes one of deciding which AFIs should have the highest priority for inclusion in the next annual operating plan or business plan to be cascaded from the strategic plan – particularly if there is a backdrop of severe financial constraints as there has been in many developing countries where I have worked.

My own preference, then, is to continue to think that 'the vision thing' or as clear an idea as possible about 'direction' is really important; but to underline the fact that one needs a good systems thinking model to help frame this vision and to justify the process of progress towards it in meaningful terms that are grounded in the potential for operational reality, given the vagaries of the operating environment.

The issue of leadership is fundamental in all of this. I will deal with the way in which it constitutes one of the important building blocks of the balanced scorecard and, conversely, how this use of the balanced scorecard can become one of the most valuable tools in any leader's 'toolkit' in Chapters 7 and 8.

CONTENT AND CONTEXT – PLANNING VERSUS EVOLUTION

Before this we should perhaps consider the concept of content and context – of whether or not we can deduce that there are 'horses for courses', and as a result choose or appoint leaders who appear to be 'the right person in the right place at the right time' once we have a better 'handle' on where the organization is now in terms of how well fitted it is to survive or thrive in its environment. Developing this idea we could consider if, on the other hand, such individuals tend to emerge anyway in these situations. This, in turn, raises the interesting question of whether leaders (or anyone else) can really plan strategy for change at all, or whether it too has a tendency simply to emerge despite, or regardless of all our best attempts to organize the future we want.

Whether you subscribe to the view that we can plan strategy, or whether you really believe that it will somehow emerge or evolve, I believe that holding to a 'living systems' view of organizations can hugely enhance the quality of your analysis and strategic thinking. Of course it is not just leaders who should think like this (whether instinctively or whether they learn the wisdom of so doing). As soon as you understand the complexity of the interdependencies in any organizational system you begin to appreciate the need for shared mental models to encourage commitment to any vision for the future of the organization. Once this complexity is understood, not only will 'binary' or linear thinking about re-engineering become an endangered species, the wisdom of the inalienable tenets famously captured in Murphy's Law will be appreciated as being part of the natural scheme of things.

Murphy's Law revisited

Murphy's Law (with my own additions in italics) informs us that:

▌ Nothing is as easy as it looks.

▌ Everything takes longer than you think it will _(but a sense of urgency and a sense of direction are vital – now more than ever before)._

▌ If anything can go wrong – it will _(especially if policy and strategy are less than feasible, because of a lack of due consideration of the SLEPT factors, or if people are determined to block it because they don't understand it or they find it threatening)._

There are, of course, ways in which we can anticipate or pre-empt Murphy's Law. They include proper attention to implementation analysis in policy planning, monitoring and evaluation, and the encouragement of a problem-predicting/problem-solving orientation among managers at all levels. Leaders must not just sell their own solutions; indeed they may sometimes have to admit to not having any if they are not themselves technocrats. They must also enthuse others about the benefits of empowerment for their own creative problem solving. This means managers and staff at all levels taking ownership of the problems and then the solutions.

Cause and effect linkages are usually what Alistair Mant calls 'ternary' – ie three-dimensional, and will usually be seen with hindsight to have effects on other parts of the system. They are rarely simply 'binary' or purely linear in their cause and effect connections. Thus there are lessons that we can learn about never falling into the dangerous and delusive complacency that logical and rigorous planning can engender about being in control of variables that one can never, in fact, control. With binary or linear thinking there is always a danger of focusing on symptomatic fixes rather than underlying causes. If, on the other hand, the whole system is constantly borne in mind throughout the planning process, and if tools such as the balanced scorecard are used to facilitate implementation analysis in strategic planning, and to frame and inform the process of monitoring and evaluation, the result will be a paradigm of 'fire prevention rather than fire fighting'.

Risk analysis and contingency planning will become less of a lottery as more of the variables and their interdependencies are routinely considered. Such a paradigm for the planning process is particularly appropriate in the context of known and common problems for both Internet start-ups and conventional businesses developing strategies for venturing into this potentially global market.

Senge (1990) said that systems thinking is partly about 'distinguishing detail complexity from dynamic complexity'. He points out that:

> *Some types of complexity are more important strategically than others. Detail complexity arises when there are many variables. Dynamic complexity arises when cause and effect are distant in time and space, and when the consequences over time of interventions are subtle and not obvious to many participants in the system. The leverage in most management situations lies in understanding dynamic complexity, not detail complexity.*

A final caveat is necessary here. Both Drucker and Minzberg have pointed out wisely that neither analysis nor planning (although invaluable) is strategy. Minzberg says: 'Because analysis is not synthesis, strategic planning is not strategy formation.'

We will explore the differences in the forthcoming chapters and provide some tools to help join these four disciplines into a coherent process for which all leaders should take responsibility, and from which extraordinary leaders can leverage extraordinary results.

3

Leadership, management and extraordinary challenges

The job of management is not supervision but leadership. . . The required transformation of the Western style of management requires that managers be leaders.

W Edwards Deming

EFFECTIVENESS AND EFFICIENCY

Leaders have to manage, but some leaders are not particularly efficient managers. Many managers are not effective leaders. There are, in fact, important differences between *efficiency* and *effectiveness*, which help us to distinguish between those characteristics required of leaders, as opposed to those required of managers. Leadership is mostly about effectiveness. It is about doing the right things (and knowing how to prioritize them). Good management is also dependent on this competence, but it is largely about efficiency. To be efficient, managers must often decide the best way to do things right; but only at more senior levels do they have to decide what are the right things to do in the first place, and particularly when times are seemingly uncertain and when permanent competitive urgency requires brave – perhaps instinctive – decisions. Leaders do not have to know all the answers but they do need to ask the right questions to help them to make strategic choices.

A good example of this would be a chief executive (or possibly a more junior but imaginative 'intrapreneur') who, while not necessarily being a technocrat, recognizes the undeniable importance of asking questions about the implications of e-business for their organization, and its continued prospects for competitiveness in marketplaces which seem increasingly to be dominated by information and communications technology (ICT). I will address some of the challenges of e-strategy formulation later in this chapter.

VALUES AND VISION

At the highest level, someone – or more usually some group of key individuals – has to define or articulate the values in which the organization or business purports to believe (and which should govern its behaviour, responsibilities and accountabilities). To guide actions which are congruent with these values, they then have to conceive and communicate a vision for a future state of being for the organization that is in line with their concept of values, and communicate it widely and clearly, ensuring that it is shared and endorsed by key stakeholders. Finally they have to facilitate the changes that the 'journey' from the present to the future will usually necessitate. In short they must steward the translation of vision into action. This is the role of leadership.

INFLUENCE AND LEARNING

The question arises, of course, whether good leaders, who can do this while taking responsibility for the complex dynamic discussed in Chapter 1 – that of managing performance and uncertainty at the same time – are therefore ever 'ordinary', or whether they have to be essentially 'extraordinary'. I have already remarked that I have yet to see an example of a so-called 'self-managing' team doing anything other than staying within its comfort zone (unless someone drags them out of it and spurs them on to greater things). Perhaps this is why we can accept the concept of a self-managing team sorting out and organizing the ordinary tasks of management, but not quite so easily that of a team that is 'self-leading'. Somehow it seems to be a contradiction in terms, and yet by rights it shouldn't be if we accept that good leaders will only ever maintain their authority and legitimacy by consensus anyway. The way they do this must essentially involve their ability to use their influence to catalyse individual and organizational learning.

Major change always involves discomfort for some, if not the majority of employees and partner organizations. The benefits of the promised future state have to be seen to be worth the short-term pain. Many stakeholders and most employees will often need to be convinced of this. The ability to be convincing in such circumstances requires influence in the form of an ability to encourage and develop others', and eventually the organization's, learning. A leader has, in effect, to be a champion of the vision and a coach and mentor to others who are struggling to relate to it. This is a long way removed from the command and direction of the traditional management approach.

COMPETENCIES FOR EXTRAORDINARY LEADERSHIP INFLUENCE

I will deal at length with the issue of how we can develop leadership competence in Chapter 13. For now let us revisit some of the competencies that we have already mentioned when discussing the nature of leadership influence. We have already identified at various points so far in this book that this range of competencies (which are related to, and spring from 'multiple intelligences' as described by Howard Gardener and Alistair Mant) should include the following 12 abilities:

1. The ability to hold the dynamic tension between the need to manage performance and uncertainty at the same time. In fact there are a number of other dynamics or dilemmas that also frequently have to be managed and we will consider these later.

2. The ability to manage others' discomfort and their risk aversion, providing constant reassurance in times of turbulence and threatening change. This ability includes that of holding another form of creative tension – that between a vision of the future and the current reality which is seen (at least by the leadership) to be undesirable or unsustainable.

3. The ability to leverage team synergy so that the whole is greater than the sum of the parts.

4. The ability to identify connections where they are not obvious (for example in the operating environment) and promote connectivity of processes and initiatives.

5. The ability to recognize (and help others recognize) the 'big picture', both in systems thinking terms and in terms of enhancing the chances of long-term sustainability of performance improvement and change initiatives.

6. The ability to apply and encourage competence in an ethical context.

7. The ability to demonstrate and role model infectious self-confidence that is born of a blend of experience and expertise.

8. The ability to enthuse others about the benefits of empowerment and of accepting ownership of problems and their solutions.

9. An obvious aptitude for continuous learning – often through acceptance of calculated risks and role modelling the acceptance of ownership of problems and solutions.

10. The ability to manage 'attention, meaning, trust, and oneself' (Bennis, 1984).

11. Role modelling 'a way of being' as well as ways of doing.

12. The ability to communicate effectively and persuasively, both orally and in writing. This may include asking (as Peter Senge suggests): 'Is this vision worthy of your commitment?'

Technology optimists and pessimists

I would add another desirable competence at this point that is more of a state of mind. I refer to optimism about ICT and its potential. Modahl (2000) suggests that people divide naturally into those who are essentially optimistic about this, and those who are essentially pessimistic. The former seem, regardless of age or social background, to recognize its potential and see it as a positive force and influence in society and in their personal lives. They quickly achieve basic computer literacy and own personal computers which they regularly use for both work and leisure purposes. They use the Internet for reference and research and may even buy some goods and services (like books or travel tickets) online. They would tell you that they don't know how they ever managed without e-mail. My 84-year-old mother is a good example! The pessimists just cannot accept that there is anything in it for them. They may buy PCs for their children, or own one because someone convinced them that they should, but they probably never switch it on, and they certainly do not wish to depend on the Internet for communications.

While one may feel that it is somewhat sad that these people will miss access to so much knowledge that is now readily available in their homes at the touch of a button, it does not matter too much to society at large if many choose to opt out. Sooner or later they will catch up. For managers of 21st-century businesses or modern public services, and especially for leaders of such organizations, it is a different matter altogether. It is now difficult to see how their effectiveness or efficiency can be in any way 'up to speed' if they are not computer literate or enthusiastic about the potential of ICT and its integration into all aspects of the organizational system. I would go so far as to suggest that these are _required_ leadership competencies.

Competence describes effective behaviour or activity that is a product of the acquisition of the necessary underpinning theoretical knowledge and the opportunity to put it into practice. By putting knowledge into practice one develops a degree of skill. Furthermore, demonstrable competence in a complex discipline like skiing (or for that matter leadership) almost certainly requires mastery of a number of related and probably interdependent competencies. In the jargon of vocational education and vocational qualifications, larger 'units of competence' are made up of a number of 'elements of competence or competencies'. Simply reading a book on skiing and committing it to memory will not enable you to put the learning into effect and demonstrate any degree of competence on the piste. It is the degree of acquired _effectiveness_ that is the important arbiter of any form of competence, and this is particularly true of leadership competence. To be an effective leader one should, it seems, be able to demonstrate and apply most if not all of the above competencies to an acceptable degree.

The compact with followers – a political parallel

I use the word 'acceptable' advisedly because it is, after all, the acceptability by the 'followers' that will ultimately determine whether a leader is perceived as effective enough in the circumstances, as many a political leader would recognize, perhaps too late and often only with the benefit of hindsight. Influence can wane easily when positional power or authority are not enough to carry hearts and minds, and once it does, even a past record of extraordinary effectiveness may not be enough to sustain leaders through the crisis of confidence. Margaret Thatcher's final months as British Prime Minister offer good evidence of just such a fall from grace. Her conviction that she was right to the bitter end probably blinded her to the evidence that she had ceased to listen (and perhaps to learn quickly enough) and therefore ceased to be perceived as effective in the hearts and minds of the public and her parliamentary colleagues.

If we look down the above list of competencies and consider how Margaret Thatcher measured up, we would readily see that in most cases, and for most of her term of office, she would have scored extremely highly. She succeeded in pleasing most of the people most of the time. Furthermore, if scoring extremely highly against such a list is a measure of extraordinary leadership, we could probably conclude that she was indeed extraordinary. In fact most people, regardless of political persuasion, would have to admit that she was *prima facie* an extraordinary leader, whether one liked her style or not. Such a judgement would be regardless of her gender, and based if nothing else on her uniquely long term of democratically elected supremacy. Perhaps the exception (to ordinariness) proves the rule, and this example of proven or accepted extraordinariness will serve to endorse the accuracy or comprehensiveness of the suggested list of required attributes.

It is interesting also to consider that influence is not some form of hypnotism. The 'followers', if we can call them that, surely have to be prepared to be influenced. There is a form of compact here that will be sustained as long as there is consensus about the value that is being added to the common purpose through the dynamics of the relationship between leader and led.

Purpose

This brings us to the all-important question of purpose. In project cycle management (PCM) parlance the word 'purpose' is usually taken to have a fairly high level connotation (above 'objectives' in a hierarchy of objectives for example), but one that is generally more practically oriented and possibly more short-to-medium term than the over-arching long-term vision. It is generally less philosophical: less to do with impact or outcome, and more to do with the synthesis of outputs and objectives into a combined and quantifiable end result. The *purpose* of achieving a number of objectives would generally be in pursuit of, and a contribution to the attainment of, a vision of the future desired state of affairs. When used in the context of individuals the flavour is generally, I believe, more philosophical and more to do with people's need for a value system and correlation between their own and their organization's principles and objectives.

Employees of an organization or enterprise in general, or members of a smaller team in particular might have a whole plethora of objectives which should, if there is a sound planning framework for their activities, all contribute to the common purpose. Furthermore this 'commonality' will imply common awareness, understanding and acceptance if activities are to be purposeful. Needless to say, the more the people who have to make these contributions are given the chance to contribute to the framing or development of that vision, the more they will feel 'empowered' to be creative and innovative in their improvement of work processes to achieve it. In addition, the more they will be seen to be committed, as opposed to compliant and anonymously involved in these processes.

Consideration of the legitimate concerns of customers in all of this has, over the last decade or so, at last been elevated to the position of paramount importance that it deserves. It is no good having a vision of being the best at something if your everyday purpose is to make and sell products that do not impress customers. It is no good issuing grand sounding policy statements and politically motivated strategies for bringing services closer to the public if your 'joined-up government' policy is perceived by the voting public as not being joined up to an ethical base of good governance, or evidenced by the personal lifestyles and principles of public service leaders. Civil service bureaucracies have too often fallen into the delusion that their existence is self-serving, forgetting that their real role is to provide a service to the public who pay their salaries.

Let us follow this diversion for a little while and explore the issue of what really constitutes the difference between management and leadership in the public services – both at home and internationally.

LEADERSHIP AND MANAGEMENT IN PUBLIC SERVICES

Elected politicians tend, I suppose, to be seen as leaders by default unless or until they prove themselves to be unworthy of the mantle of leadership by failure to deliver on promises to their constituents, or failure to deliver expected standards of personal behaviour and ethical conduct in public life. They are rarely, if ever, seen as managers unless they fail in some specific task of quantifiable delivery for which they were given responsibility. The recent fall from grace or *dis*-grace of UK government minister Peter Mandelson would, no doubt, qualify on both counts: his personal financial dealings were questioned on the one hand, and his management – or mismanagement as many would have it – of London's Millennium Dome project for which he had direct responsibility, on the other.

Senior civil servants, would, I suggest, generally be seen as managers rather than leaders – at least by the public by whom, ironically, they are probably rarely seen at all! The very pursuit of anonymity, which is almost culturally sacrosanct in civil services worldwide, tends to preclude any public opportunity for overt demonstration of leadership, and yet the huge responsibilities and accountabilities of the most senior public servants would certainly qualify them in any analysis based on such criteria. Furthermore, their own subordinates would certainly see them as leaders within the service, and hugely influential in the process of governments' achievement (or otherwise) of policy objectives and manifesto promises. It follows that the best of those who were in senior positions at the time of an extraordinary political leader like Margaret Thatcher were almost certainly as extraordinary in their own leadership – if not more so given the scale of the changes that they were frequently required to manage and lead. This was in order that the political party in power (the Conservative government of the time) could deliver on its promises and rightly claim to have radically reformed the civil service in the UK. Although the credit for such reforms will always be taken by the politicians – and to be fair they usually frame the vision, set the agenda and instil the sense of urgency – the hard adaptive work of implementation usually falls to public service leaders whether or not they personally agree with the ideological aspects of the required changes.

No shareholders or stockbrokers are peering over the shoulders of public servants when they spend time and money developing methodologies to implement change. In the public services it is never quite so obvious and apparent that 'time is money'. As a result, what has happened is that surprisingly the art of leading and managing major change has often been developed to such an advanced state in the public sector, that in some aspects it now leads the way, and even the private sector is acknowledging this lead. I will deal later with some of the models that have been used and which I feel leaders in all fields can use to their advantage when extraordinary results are demanded.

LEADERSHIP AND E-STRATEGY

Public services face huge challenges in harnessing the potential of ICT in pursuit of their aim to improve service delivery and bring it closer to users. However, they are hardly at the cutting edge in the sense that commercial companies facing the challenges, opportunities or threats of the global e-commerce marketplace are.

I am not a technocrat and perhaps this is why I believe that in many cases what I have observed as a crisis of e-strategy formulation in some (and I understand it is in fact many) such companies or corporations is actually a crisis of leadership. It may also be a crisis of resources but the latter is in many ways a corollary of the former. Modahl (2000) has this to say about the requirement for leadership:

Traditional companies that have created successful Internet businesses have pursued one of three basic models: wholesale transformation of the existing business into an electronic one; a risk-balancing approach in which a separate unit seeks some outside funding; and a hands-off venture investment approach. In the end, however, all of these approaches require the direct and active support of the CEO. No Internet strategy can succeed without it.

Continuing this theme she says:

> *Winners will align their organization, funding, and leadership around the Internet Economy and Dynamic Trade. They will set aside or manage diversions such as potential channel conflict. They will fund their Internet operations fully enough to create revenue growth momentum – and they will find this funding from patient sources that can be comfortable with the risk of generating losses in the near term. The winners will assign or recruit the best people to electronic commerce and give them enough authority to challenge the old ways of doing business – and they'll do it quickly. In the end the companies that win the battle for the Internet customers will be the ones that really want to.*

One is tempted to ask, so what's different? If you remove the e-words from the quotation does it not describe or reiterate what management gurus (and for that matter the lessons of best practice) have been teaching us for decades? Does it not imply that there is nothing new under the sun when it comes to 'best practice' – in e-commerce just as in traditional business? This is because both require committed people; and the parallels underline that the vision and momentum (including perhaps a greater than ever sense of urgency in the e-business global marketplace) must come from the leadership?

Bill Gates (1999) quotes Michael Dell, who characterizes the direct business today as:

> *different combinations of face-to-face, ear-to-ear, and keyboard-to-keyboard. Each has its place. The Internet doesn't replace people. It makes them more efficient. By moving routine interactions to the Web and enabling customers to do some things for themselves, we've freed up our sales-people to do more meaningful things with customers.*

The scale, the momentum, and the pace of the implied changes are indeed great. It will therefore be those leaders who can understand their extraordinary implications and opportunities, and those who can formulate strategies which require no advanced technical knowledge but rather a visionary awareness of potential and its requirements for overall organizational systems development, who will prove successful in rising to the challenges.

Businesses trying to develop direct Web sales should never forget that the high-quality customer service that they think (possibly rightly) that they have built through their traditional operations may no longer be appropriate. A behaviour shift for both sales staff and customers may be necessary. Simplicity and convenience are paramount. Michael Dell sums this up by saying:

> *We had to build an Internet system that was so convenient, customers got more value for their time than they did on the phone. That was the only way we could wean them off face-to-face or ear-to-ear contact. It was a high bar to clear.*

The pace of change

So if strategy formulation for e-business is in essence no different from conventional strategy in terms of its key drivers and its reliance for effectiveness on people and good relationships, what are the differences, if any, in addition to the need for convenience that Michael Dell stresses? Successful e-commerce will have to be fundamentally different in one way: *speed*. The speed of developments and the rate or pace of changes require a greater than ever clarity in the vision and direction that are set out or championed by the leadership. This will normally mean a clear vision of where the Internet strategy is taking the business based on clear analysis of options and feasibility, clear decision making and clear implementation plans. Increasingly we will have to think about medium-term planning for next summer!

The digitization of warfare is now enabling weapons controllers to see further than they can shoot despite darkness or the fog of war (until recently and without the latest technology the opposite was true). As a result of technological advances commanders in bunkers under the Pentagon can watch in real time as their warplanes deliver high-tech laser-guided weapons with surgical accuracy into a designated window in a building in Baghdad. Commercial companies are already experimenting with being able to offer to relay video coverage of your family party or wedding to your friends and relations on the other side of the world in real time. The international news media have been doing this for a while. Given this immediacy there will now be much less time for leaders to indulge in the luxury of lengthy reflection. The passport office in Holland has cut the time of issuing a passport from days to hours by offering a Web-based service. Satellite linked videoconferencing can already facilitate virtual meetings of business leaders in different continents without the need for international travel. Global distance learning centres funded by the World Bank are now able to offer the same technology for the support of distance learning in some of the poorest of developing countries.

The supplier or resource partner is becoming fundamentally important in these accelerated product and service delivery processes. In fact I would suggest that for our purposes we should regard these partnerships very much as 'teams'. Organizations which appear on the face of it to be the 'front' for e-business or Web-based services are frequently not the producer, and often may not even hold any inventory. They take the lead in a team venture and model the latest form of leadership by acting as facilitator of the synergy of processes. Every Dell computer is customized. As a result their delivery system has to depend on complete synergy of all related systems and 'just-in-time' delivery – both of components and of the finished product. The coherence of the overall system has to be complete and one of the significant responsibilities of leadership has to be sustaining the balance between team maintenance and individual needs of team members in this team effort to achieve the task.

It appears that the first leadership 'guru' in the management training field, and the first ever to hold a professorial chair of leadership studies at a UK university, John Adair, had it right when he invented the concept of an action-centred leadership model. Adair's model highlights the mutual interdependence of these three components (task, team maintenance and individual needs). We will explore this further in the next chapter.

Part II

Charting the course

4

The view from the tower

Who needs to learn what to develop, understand, commit to, and implement the strategy?

Ronald Heifetz

GETTING UP INTO THE TOWER

Heifetz and Laurie (1997) identified the fact that leadership should be both active and reflective. They suggested that leaders have to alternate between participating and observing and they have to develop an instinct for knowing when to put themselves into or out of the action. The authors urged business leaders to 'get on the balcony' to help them see the overall picture, and to be in a better position 'to identify the adaptive challenge' that it poses. Adaptive challenges are those that require new and innovative solutions that cannot be developed or delivered with a 'business as usual' attitude. Once they are identified, people will often rise to the challenge of finding solutions if they are encouraged to do so.

If one thinks of either standing in the middle of a busy airport, or alternatively viewing the scene from the control tower, one can immediately understand the difference in perspective that the two viewpoints can give. I like this analogy because it extends the metaphor of planning a journey and charting the required course. Heifetz and Laurie make use of sporting similes and quote examples of how many of the greatest team sports stars seem to have the ability to read the pattern of the game even while on the pitch and in the thick of things. Perhaps this ability is part of what makes them extraordinary in their field.

Further analogies

The analogy of the dance is also another way to look at this. When one is engaged in a dance and in the centre of the floor, it is not possible to get any proper sense of the patterns made by everyone else in the room. Motion, and even the noise, makes observation difficult. Indeed it is possible that one's attention will be captured by the music, as it should be if one is participating as a dancer. In this case one will need to concentrate on one's partner, and have a sense of the space needed by this person and anyone else dancing nearby in order not to tread on their toes. To discern the longer patterns on the floor – and to see who is dancing with whom, in what groups, in what way, and who is sitting out and for which kinds of dance – we would have to step off the floor and get up onto the balcony. Perhaps it can even provide a sanctuary where we can hear ourselves think.

For effective and efficient control of air traffic, there is clearly only one place to be – up in the tower. Here all the tools are provided to facilitate the overview as well as the decision making, but no one would call this a sanctuary. Indeed it can be quite a stressful place to be! Similar complexity and the extraordinary pace of e-business are already, as we saw in the last chapter, affording leaders less time for the luxury of reflection, whether it be from the tower, the balcony, the touch-line or anywhere else.

Getting 'up into the tower' or 'onto the balcony' should nevertheless create space for a leader to interpret trends which otherwise could have been undetectable and which could possibly have swept him or her away. This may be particularly true when wrestling with issues concerning entrenched cultural paradigms or trying to manage the stress of actually getting real adaptive work done by others in the organization. It is not a place, however, for retreating from the issues. It should provide space for diagnostic review, which in turn should enable action planning. Perhaps the greatest leaders – the most *extraordinary* leaders – do have the ability to dance and at the same time read the pattern of the dance. Like the greatest sports people they seem to have the ability to read the pattern of the game while they are playing. Like great generals, they seem to be able to see through the 'fog of war'. Such ability can lead to great wins and extraordinary success, but it is rare. Perhaps this ability is a 'gift' and is innate. Perhaps it cannot be taught; but perhaps a predisposition for learning it can and does exist in those who grow into the role of being extraordinary leaders. Perhaps it is the aptitude for lifelong learning and the constant innovative application of it to new complex challenges that is the 'gift'. For those who posses it the best service they can provide to their organizations is to endeavour to encourage it where they detect signs of it in others.

Seeing the whole system

In Chapter 1 I referred to Alistair Mant's book *Intelligent Leadership* and his metaphor of 'the frog and the bicycle'. It may seem obvious, and perhaps common sense to those who have a natural proclivity for what has become known as 'systems thinking' (and this number, it seems to me, includes a minority of men and the majority of women), that any complex organization must, by definition, be more like a living organism (a frog) than a mechanical device (a bicycle). Unfortunately the sense has proved to be far from common, and its scarcity has consequently failed to deter numerous disastrous and near-fatal 're-engineering' attempts.

The whole system should be taken to mean not just the organizational structure in purely functional or two-dimensional terms (as in an organization chart), but also the complex multi-dimensional amalgam of values, policies, strategies, practices, processes, resources and relationships. One cannot necessarily expect immediately to get a clear picture of all of these and the dynamics of their interdependencies by getting up onto the balcony or into the tower, but it certainly helps – especially as the picture from this vantage point becomes clearer over time. In a purely mechanical metaphor one could imagine that observation might reveal 'where the wheels are squeaking'. With the living systems perspective one might hope to gain some insight into why, and possibly into what effect this was having on the general health of the organization. The chances are that staff on the ground will often know perfectly well both where and why the wheels are squeaking, but may not feel it is worth volunteering the information unless they are specifically asked, or unless it is generally understood that such involvement is welcome, expected and recognized.

THE LEARNING ORGANIZATION

The concept of collective intelligence has been around for a long time. As children at primary school we were probably first introduced to it in the context of the behaviour of bees, wasps and ants as 'social' organisms that seemed to build and share a body of common 'learning' that resulted in the whole colony being somehow more than the sum of its parts. The way in which this learning produces a fitness for role has interesting links to evolution theory. The concept has found favour more recently in organizational development and management studies through the work of Peter Senge and others who have highlighted the importance of building 'learning organizations'. The thinking is that only organizations that can learn fast will be equipped for the period of rapid change in which we have found ourselves at the turn of the century and the start of a new millennium. Heifetz and Laurie state firmly that: 'Solutions to adaptive challenges reside not in the executive suite but in the collective intelligence of employees at all levels.'

It is probably not easy to prove conclusively but I would suggest that the development of collective intelligence is far more likely to be a product of a holistic corporate 'health and fitness regime' than the result of radical surgery or forced marriage in the form of a hostile takeover. Furthermore, I would take issue very slightly with Heifetz and Laurie, and say that while the solutions to most adaptive challenges do not reside in the executive suite, responsibility for encouraging employees at all levels to feel free to use their collective intelligence, through overt sponsorship of such a 'health and fitness regime', certainly does.

THE LEADER AS PART OF THE SYSTEM

By suggesting that leaders should step back occasionally to get a proper overview of the system, I am not suggesting (and I am sure that Heifetz and Laurie were not suggesting) that leaders should in any sense ever see themselves as divorced from it, or that they are not intrinsically a part of it. The creative tension that should exist between leaders and the organization is paralleled in that which exists between their vision – or more accurately the shared vision leaders must help to build and steward – and current reality. According to Senge, the creative tension is the integrating principle, and leaders are in fact responsible for organizational learning.

In Chapter 2, I introduced the EFQM Excellence Model as an example of a balanced scorecard model for analysis when attempting to prioritize the vital performance and service delivery improvements that organizations must identify across all elements of their overall system if they are to remain competitive and customer focused. This is the most practical of systems-thinking tools and its purpose is to facilitate exactly what is described here: organizational learning through continuous improvement in which leadership plays a fundamental role. I shall deal more fully with its practical application in the Extraordinary Leader's Toolkit in Chapter 8.

BALANCING PERFORMANCE AND CHANGE MANAGEMENT

Just as efforts to improve organizational performance must consider and seek out ways to do this in all parts of the organizational system, there must be recognition that change and the turbulence it generates will undoubtedly affect all parts of the system. This is why it is one of the fundamental tasks of leadership to balance attention to the management of performance with attention to the management of change or uncertainty. Often attention that is directed at performance improvement is focused on improving the skills and abilities of individuals and there is much merit in this. It is often more productive than assuming that there is some magic formula by which processes can be re-engineered without investment in, or consultation with the people who have to run them. The really clever trick is to combine the two ideas and facilitate continuous process improvement through the personal competence development and empowerment of those who have to manage these processes.

Opportunities for personal development should, of course, be motivating and they often are. The best way to improve proper understanding of an organization's needs and strategic objectives, and at the same time to develop personal commitment to these, however, is to focus on results, and to hold people accountable for achieving the desired outcomes of their individual work contributions. Achievement in this context is often not as conveniently finite as one would like in terms of its measurability, but results are almost always easier to quantify than the results of associated initiatives. For example, trying to measure the impact that training may have on process improvements or even competence is notoriously difficult. Furthermore, if care is exercised in the definition and agreement of specific, measurable, agreed, realistic and time-bound (SMART) objectives at the strategic level, these can usually be broken down and cascaded to all levels of employee responsibility.

RESULTS-ORIENTED MANAGEMENT

Having made an appeal for systems thinking it may seem paradoxical to add that there may be overall systemic advantage in the development of appraisal instruments that are quite simply only about whether or not agreed objectives or results are achieved at all levels in organizations. The integration into the assessment of complex variables that attempt to cover a whole range of competencies, and somehow integrate the assessment, rating or ranking of performance in both 'process' and 'results' areas, perhaps even with links to pay, usually leads to abuse, or at best misunderstanding of the instrument. The appraisal system can fall into disrepute and be resented, and it can endanger the wider performance management system of which it should be just one element or tool. I will deal at greater length with the issue of best practice in performance appraisal in Chapter 12. Suffice it to say here that it is only ever as good as the will of senior managers to take it seriously and to use it objectively to monitor and evaluate both individual and team progress towards the achievement of desired results. There have to be some incentives for achievement and some sanctions for failure, if this failure occurs despite all reasonable agreements and attempts to equip employees to achieve their objectives through training and development.

It is the leadership of all the enabling processes that counts. This includes the identification and prioritizing of the vital few areas for operational improvement that are needed (or that can be realistically afforded and cascaded into individual objectives) at any time. Such management of performance improvement (which takes into account the uncertainty of the road to the future) will provide an environment that is best able to empower employees to optimize their individual potential, and to align and achieve their agreed personal and corporate objectives and results targets. The role of performance management is to provide systems that support what leaders are doing to nurture the whole system. It is not rocket science and the tools are not engineering tools. In fact, if anything, they are more like a gardener's tools in this context of nurturing future growth.

ACTION-CENTRED LEADERSHIP

Back in the mid-1960s John Adair developed one of the most enduring of leadership models, his theory of action-centred leadership. The model in simple form consists of three overlapping circles representing the task, the need for team maintenance, and concern for the individual needs of team members. It was, in fact, a simple systems thinking model which probably accounts for its continued relevance, even though some aspects of the associated theory that Adair developed may now be seen by some as perhaps a little 'old fashioned' in their primary task orientation.

They were certainly right for their time and for the context in which they were first developed, which was the military one. The essential message was that achievement of the task could be prejudiced if due attention was not simultaneously placed on actions to maintain the cohesion and morale of the team, and actions to take cognizance of the strengths or weaknesses of individual team members. I was one of John Adair's students at the time when he developed these ideas at the Royal Military Academy, Sandhurst, and the soundness and elegant simplicity of the theory has, for me, stood the test of time well.

The means and methods that a leader might choose to employ today to identify and prioritize tasks and communicate urgency and import-ance to others have undoubtedly changed and developed over the last 30 years. Understanding of the issues surrounding best practice for 'team maintenance' has improved immeasurably, as has the nature of what it is reasonable for individuals to expect in terms of recognition of the importance of their personal needs as well as rights. In general,

for leaders to be seen as being rightly more sensitive to these considerations than perhaps previous generations were, the style of leadership
has had to change more than the substance. All we probably need
to do to bring John Adair's model up to date is to include a wider
range of 'stakeholders' and partnership interests when considering
what we mean by the 'team', and a wider range of results areas –
including considerations of customer or client satisfaction and continuous improvement – in our definition of the 'task'. This is basically
what the various balanced scorecard models (as originally pioneered
by Kaplan and Norton) attempt to do.

Considering suppliers as 'partners', and seeking a 'win-win' formula
for maximizing joint productivity and profitability through a 'just-in-
time' (JIT) delivery system has for some time been fashionably popular
in line with a general recognition that relationship procurement and
relationship marketing make sense in financial terms. Web-based sales
and service companies have come to realize that such systems are
essential for sustaining the pace of supply if the unprecedented demand
that the Internet can generate is to be met. Computerized solutions are
now marketed to help managers keep pace with the volume of data
and transactions that e-business generates, and rightly so. Managers
and especially leaders must recognize, however, that such information
technology resources are not, and never will be, a substitute for the
clarity of vision, and the alignment of funding and organization that
only the highest quality human resources in the form of leadership can
provide.

5

Keeping the traffic moving – and the signals clear

Never confuse motion with action.

Ernest Hemingway

THE VITAL PRIORITIES

Once leaders have identified the dimensions of the organizational problems that require adaptive work (by asking the right questions and noting system connections), the challenge is to keep attention focused and identify priorities among the issues that need attention. Sometimes – indeed quite often – a seemingly marginal or secondary issue will only capture the attention of a small minority who can see from their position that it is important or even critical. Even an issue that on the one hand is clearly not marginal by any stretch of the imagination – like the impact of the Internet and e-commerce – may only be seen as critical and urgent by a few managers within an organization.

Bill Gates (1999) describes how the impetus for Microsoft's response to the Internet didn't come from him or from other senior executives:

It came from a small number of dedicated employees who saw events unfolding. Through our electronic systems they were able to rally everybody to their cause. Their story exemplifies our policy, from day one, that smart people anywhere in the company should have the power to drive an initiative.

Such 'intrapreneurs' may not always be so lucky. They may lose sleep over what they should do about convincing others of their insight. The task for them is to draw attention to it, often in the face of resistance by the larger community (or perhaps the most senior management) who have other concerns.

One of the leadership responsibilities here is to decide, or lead the process of consensus to decide, what is and what is not strategically important in the medium term and how, therefore, to prioritize activities for operations in the shorter-term operational or business plans. Many managers, when first attempting to apply tried and tested tools for better personal time management or time planning, make a dangerous mistake. They conclude erroneously that by making lists every day of tasks to be done (and in particular by identifying which of these are both urgent and important), they will be planning their time efficiently and making decisions more effectively.

Wrong! Doing this – especially in a hierarchical organization where decision making is usually pushed 'upstairs' – leads to a situation where senior managers have so many tasks to do every day which qualify as both urgent and important that they never have time for the ones that are important but not necessarily urgent. These are normally the big jobs concerning big issues – the ones that keep being put off – and the ones that will result in greater crises and the need for more and more crisis management and 'fire fighting' if they are not dealt with incrementally. We are talking about the ability to prioritize over time. Directors of successful but small growing businesses are often too busy dealing with the management and resourcing of current projects for which they are responsible, and looking to develop these into more of the same with existing clients or markets. Frequently they do not have time to 'get up into the tower' and take the overview of what might be emerging as exciting new opportunities for new business development or partnerships. Often they do not have the time to listen to the very people that they brought into the growing business for this purpose.

A parable for our times

I am reminded of a wonderful story, given to me by an Indian colleague and e-business expert, Sanjay Saxena, that illustrates this with a typically Asian and almost philosophical parable. A guru was using props to illustrate the nature of the problem of life management and the need to prioritize in a fundamental way. He took a large pitcher and filled it up with big stones until there was clearly room for no more. His audience all agreed that it was indeed full to the brim. He then took smaller stones and proceeded to get quite a few of them into the pitcher as they slipped down among the bigger stones. Then he added even smaller stones in the form of gravel and the pitcher was able to absorb a surprising amount, much to the amusement of the audience. Handfuls of sand were then added slowly until all agreed that the vessel really was now completely full. As a final flourish, the guru added water until it was seen to come right to the brim. 'What do you suppose the moral of this demonstration is?' asked the teacher. Knowing that the subject of the lecture seemed to be efficiency in planning one's time, there was general agreement that the lesson to be learnt was that there was always time to cram more tasks than you ever thought possible into a day. 'No,' said the Guru, 'the moral is that you must get the big stones in first!'

While this ability is important for the efficiency of individual managers, it is central to the whole strategic and operational planning process, and thus to the effectiveness of leadership. It can be instinctive but it can also be learnt and there are a number of excellent models to guide leaders in an optimum approach to the process.

THE EXTRAORDINARY LEADERSHIP TOOLKIT

The best models are those (like the one in the story) that stress the importance of a 'process' centred approach to the leadership and management of change (and paradigm shift) as a whole, and sign the route for the management of the work that will bring it about. They underline the fact that holistic systems thinking (seeing and considering the whole integrated picture – as from the tower) should underpin the more linear project cycle management processes (and tools) that are necessary for actual implementation of adaptive action plans. The key models that I have chosen to feature are those that I have found to be both insightful and practical in their applicability to real-life situations and change programmes in both private and public sectors. If nothing else they will serve as good checklists and *aide-memoirs* for practitioners such as consultants, as well as being (when taken together) a proven and reliable toolkit for leaders to use to guide the direction, process, and necessary framework of major change efforts.

An eight-stage process of leading major change (adapted from the original conceived by John Kotter, 1999) is the first model I have chosen to include in the toolkit. The Mindworks Approach – a user-friendly (ie no 'consultant-speak') strategic thinking process tool for guiding management teams through the medium-term planning process – will be featured in the next chapter. Analysis and planning are no substitutes for strategy and action, but a cycle of careful planning which will surely be much shorter than the traditional process is now evidently and particularly important in the new age of e-commerce where, according to Robin Tye, E-business Lead Partner at PricewaterhouseCoopers (quoted by Modahl, 2000):

> *An e-business year is about three months. Instead of looking at the past and projecting, what you do is identify the key drivers of change and look at scenarios depending on what those drivers do. You have to ask lots of what ifs.*

The Mindworks Approach that we shall consider in Chapter 6 will help us to do this.

The EFQM's Excellence Model will be introduced in Chapter 7 as the next part of the 'toolkit'. This is the example of a balanced scorecard methodology first introduced in Chapter 2. It clarifies how excellent performance results, customer satisfaction and motivated employees can be the product of coordinated attention to continuous improvement across a range of five enabler criteria: leadership, policy and strategy, processes, human resource management, and resources (which include, as we have already seen, partnerships with suppliers or distributors).

A further two strategic and operational/project planning models will feature in Chapter 10 to complete the Extraordinary Leadership Toolkit. The first models to be introduced are essentially strategic in nature. That is to say they help you to 'get up into the tower' to take the higher level overview so that you can relate to the importance of the sequence of the process of leading major change and the strategic thinking that is necessary to programme the required planning. They also facilitate systems thinking and attention to interdependencies and connectivity. Later models deal with the more operational aspects of project cycle management and the team leadership that will be required to prioritize and to empower others to accept responsibility and accountability for achievement, and for alignment of their own objectives with those of the organization as a whole.

A MODEL FOR THE PROCESS OF LEADING MAJOR CHANGE

Rarely has a book rung bells with me, reflecting my own personal experience, as clearly and as immediately as Harvard Professor John Kotter's very personal 1999 offering, _Leading Change_. Kotter starts by identifying eight reasons for the frequent failure of major corporate change programmes. We have all encountered them! He then turns these around and, devoting a chapter to each, he highlights how addressing them in sequence (and this is the important point) can afford the best chance of making change efforts sustainable, and the best chance of their resulting in a new paradigm or way of doing business. He does not underestimate the scale of the challenge or its difficulty, but he is at pains to point out that the fundamental groundwork has to be done first. The ground has, as it were, to be secured before people parachute in with the latest weapons, tools and technology. In fact – you have to get the big stones in first! To continue with the military metaphor: if you fail to secure the ground in the early stages of the campaign, you will find yourself fighting numerous rearguard actions and skirmishes because of the appearance of elements of resistance which were originally undetected, underestimated, or not effectively neutralized. Here is Kotter's model of the eight-stage process, with very slight modifications of my own.

An eight-stage process for leading major change

1. Establishing a sense of urgency

▌ Examining the supply/demand relationship realities and operating environment.

▌ Identifying threats and opportunities.

▌ Programming the process – identifying priorities and key stakeholder interests.

2. Creating the guiding coalition

▌ Putting together a group of key individuals with enough power and commitment to lead the changes.

3. Developing the vision and strategy

▌ Creating a vision to help direct the change efforts.

▌ Developing policies, strategies and systems for achieving that vision.

4. Communicating the change vision

▌ Using every means possible to communicate the new vision and strategy constantly to all stakeholders.

▌ Having leaders and senior managers role model the behaviour expected of managers and employees.

5. Empowering broad-based action

▌ Getting rid of obstacles.

▌ Changing systems or structures that undermine the vision.

▌ Using systems thinking to improve processes.

▌ Encouraging risk taking and non-traditional ideas, activities and actions.

6. Generating quick wins

▌ Planning for visible measurable improvements.

▌ Creating these wins (not just hoping they will happen).

▌ Recognizing and finding ways of rewarding those who make them possible.

7. Consolidating gains and producing more change

▌ Using increased credibility to change all systems, structures and policies that don't fit the vision or fit together.

▌ Hiring, promoting and developing people who can make it happen.

▌ Reinvigorating the process with new projects, themes and change agents.

8. Anchoring new approaches in the culture

▌ Performance improvement through benchmarked 'productivity' and customer-focused behaviour.

▌ Articulating connections between new behaviours and success.

▌ Developing the means for leadership development and succession.

I will take each of Kotter's stages in turn and add a few remarks based on my personal experience of putting this process into practice in complex and difficult operating environments – both unconsciously before, and then after I had first seen this model and found that it mirrored my own reality.

1. Establishing a sense of urgency

First it is probably worth mentioning that all change programmes are by definition 'projects', or made up of a number of component projects; that is to say they are constrained by both time and resources – particularly budget. You cannot have a project that goes on indefinitely without prescribed financial limits. This is a contradiction in terms, although in some organizations there may be a vested interest in projects being repeatedly and indefinitely extended; this is something to guard against because the necessary sense of urgency will not exist. The interesting thing is that increasingly businesses have to be run more like a succession of projects than as vocations, because of the all-pervading sense of urgency that is necessary to cope with the pace of change and the required speed of reaction.

The issue of supply and demand realities is significant. If there is no demand for a newer or better service, how can we expect anyone to sign up to the necessity of providing it? The word 'realities' is important here, however. The realities of the marketplace are themselves changing rapidly and may often be different to traditional perceptions of the mechanics or dynamics of supply and demand. An analysis of stakeholders' interests and of the relative strengths of both their opinions and their influence is vital. Sometimes new and creative methods will need to be devised to conduct such an analysis where conventional wisdom seems itself to be a victim of change. For example, it has become apparent in the last three years of pioneering e-commerce and Web-based sales, that consumer groups do not fit the traditional patterns. Take my 84-year-old mother who, as I mentioned earlier, is definitely a technology 'optimist'. Her enthusiasm for the medium of the Internet and her access through it to a global market completely belies any classification of her as a relatively housebound 'little old lady', or I suggest any other conventional marketing classifications. This new 'science' of e-market analysis and segmentation has become known as 'technographics' and we will return to some of its lessons later. It is, of course, not an exact science.

When Bennis (1984) writes of the 'management of attention' by leaders he says: 'They communicate an extraordinary focus of commitment, which attracts people to them. . . [They] manage attention through a compelling vision that brings others to a place they have not been before.' I think this is true but it seems at first sight to endorse a rather traditional view of the leader being expected to have the solution and sell it. So perhaps the compelling vision that Bennis refers to here is actually not so much the ultimate vision of the future for the organization, but rather a clearer vision than that of most people of how to get there – for the change process that according to Kotter must be led and not simply managed. It is the management of attention (through the compelling vision), which brings people to a new place and a new realization or paradigm.

Kotter seems to be saying that the sense of urgency must precede and perhaps be the catalyst for the definition of the vision, but he is talking about the vision or goal that leaders of the organization have for its change programme. It is the ability to communicate this in what Bennis calls a 'compelling' way that helps to create the sense of urgency. The leader's task here can, of course, be greatly assisted if there is a crisis or a hugely exciting brand new opportunity that 'compels' attention. If the sword of Damocles (perhaps in the form of bankruptcy) is poised inches above people's heads they will normally concede that something needs to be done to raise it. The threat of being hanged (as Dr Johnson famously remarked) concentrates minds wonderfully but only, I suggest, if it is the threat of being hanged – as he went on to say – in the morning! Furthermore, the raising of the sword must be permanent despite the fact that I have often seen the sense of urgency evaporate the minute the immediate threat receded. In such cases care must be taken to reinvigorate the process with new challenges that replace the original motivation of pure survival.

2. Creating the guiding coalition

Kotter's terminology is interesting here. He talks of the necessity to 'create' the guiding coalition and 'put together' a group of key influential individuals. This implies a proactive leadership responsibility (in the chief executive sense) or alternatively a significant role here for a change agent who must show equally extraordinary leadership perceptiveness and skills of persuasion, although he or she may not have positional power or authority over the whole programme. Consultants can often fulfil this function and will usually bring the benefit of 'the immigrant's eye' to the situation – a detachment of perspective that the leader can find both fresh and stimulating to their own creative train of thought.

The selection of this 'guiding coalition' may be partly dictated by the need to include obvious key stakeholders purely by dint of their positional power and authority and perhaps regardless of the strength of their own convictions at the outset. This has to happen in cases where the pertaining politics or protocol will simply not permit their exclusion, for example in public service reform programmes that demand the demonstrable 'ownership' of politicians and the highest ranking civil servants. It is helpful if both the power and the commitment are in place; they will need to be eventually. Initially it is the power and authority and at least the preparedness to communicate the sense of urgency that are needed. Passive endorsement and permission to proceed with the treatment can be nurtured and developed into proactive commitment provided that the need for political expediency is always understood. Perhaps if the edict _carpe diem_ (seize the day, or the moment) is always borne in mind, the demands of politics (which of course are often as much about 'the power and the glory' as they are about power and commitment), can be channelled and harnessed to good effect. Pragmatism of this nature is just as necessary in major corporate change programmes as it is in the public sector.

Just as it is important proactively to create the guiding coalition, it is also important in my experience to engage the active and visible participation of its members once it is formed. As we have seen, it may be necessary on occasion for pragmatic reasons to have token representation of the 'ruling elite' but it is to be discouraged. People are rightly sensitive to the messages (both positive and negative) that role modelling can send out. Delivery of high-level messages about policy and strategy for major change cannot be delegated to change agents or consultants, although the latter can often advise on their content and timing. Policy advisers may draft papers or even speeches but the politicians have to deliver them with clearly communicated ownership and enthusiasm that is perceived as genuine by the public, or customers for services like the business community or civil society groups.

Senior civil servants may then subsequently have to lead and role model the internal changes that are necessary to facilitate service improvement and delivery of the promise, but the public will only be aware of the external impact or outcome of these improved processes and behaviours. These in turn must be seen as congruent with the political promises if the whole change process is to be credible and its results sustainable. When politicians now talk about 'joined-up government' they should bear in mind that it is these connections that are fundamental. Once they are understood, the more practical implications for better access (perhaps through single points of service, one-stop shops, or even the Internet) can be identified and dealt with. The same pattern should be evident in commercial companies or corporations in terms of the fulfilment of promises about quality and service delivery living up to brand image and the customers' definition of 'value for money'. If the 'quality' and 'excellence' movements have achieved anything, it has been to erase the distinction in people's minds that the public and private sectors are fundamentally different in this respect. It really comes down, in either case, to organizational and individual values underpinning both the direction and the activity of day-to-day operations. The guiding coalition must personify and exemplify this.

3. Developing the vision and strategy

I spoke earlier about the need for clarity of direction, as indicated by a compass, being more important (certainly at the strategic level) than a detailed road map. The latter can afford to be flawed in small ways and will usually prove to be so. The former cannot afford flaws. It cannot afford errors in the definition of direction or in the reasoning on which this is established. Having said this we should always recognize that while hindsight may be 20–20, foresight is not. A vision is largely about a future that will always be over the horizon and beyond our absolute control. Its achievement cannot be guaranteed at the outset and its parameters may have to be iteratively changed with the benefit of hindsight as time passes to ensure that its stays within reach. To make it as credible and durable as possible, therefore, it should be as immutable as possible, through being based on immutable values, while not appearing to be a string of platitudes or a socio-economic wish list.

This is a bit of a juggling act. There are dynamic tensions, dilemmas and conundrums in these requirements. Consequently neither the guiding coalition, nor its ultimate leadership, nor its advisers should expect the creation of a vision necessarily to be a quick fix. In my experience it often takes a lot of brainstorming and analysis before the synthesis of a good distilled statement is possible. I will not divert at this point into a lengthy discussion of what constitutes a good vision statement. The important issue at stake here is that of the guiding coalition's responsibility to achieve consensus about the vision's clarity and the credibility of its potential for achievement in the medium term – or however much time is available for the change process. This is one of the 'big stones' that must be put in first. Anything beyond this will probably be out of focus at the present time but the speed of change of the operating environment will dictate that the leadership must constantly try to pull that focus as an indicator of whether overall progress is on course and whether, in fact, the chosen course remains the right one.

Credibility and achievability are as much, if not more, about strategy as they are about vision and policy. The vision and the policies capture the main 'whats' and perhaps the 'where' of our picture of the future. Strategy is the 'how'. The guiding coalition must consider high-level strategy and determine the main 'hows' with some attempt at risk assessment. Development of lower level 'hows' to exploit opportunities or overcome barriers will be the job of management when they develop operational plans for the shorter term. A vision statement may say, for example, that an organization aspires to espouse change in order to contribute more fully to the overall socio-economic welfare of society through adherence to the highest standards of quality and service delivery. Before saying this one needs to think about how this will be done and whether or not it is feasible and achievable in a time frame that is long enough to be strategic but short enough to capture attention and endorse the sense of urgency. 'Fine words', as the old English proverb reminds us, 'butter no parsnips'. They cannot be a substitute for action, and they must not be an excuse for inaction because they were too ambitious in the first place.

4. Communicating the change vision

Good communication usually involves more than one delivery method. Lectures are more likely to be interesting, and thus more likely to facilitate learning, if the lecturer uses a variety of visual aids or, perhaps when the session is an extended workshop, if there is more than one facilitator.

It is incumbent on leaders, and I include here the whole guiding coalition or executive team, to think creatively about how they can maximize the chances of the message getting across and being taken seriously by all concerned with the change effort. They need to be prepared to communicate the vision and the key strategies loudly and clearly so that nobody will be in any doubt that this is going to happen. There must be no room for doubt that employees had better take it seriously, and that their full support and enthusiastic enrolment in the adaptive work of making changes happen are expected and will be appreciated, recognized and rewarded. Professional advice on information management or public relations may be useful in this exercise but ultimately it will be the substance and perceptions that are generated about integrity rather than the style or 'spin' that matters.

The fashion now in highly developed corporate environments is to try to move forward rapidly on all fronts, on the assumption that real empowerment of workers to change little things and processes because they see the benefits that should accrue, will be more effective than any form of more traditional top-down driving of the changes. The role of leadership in this new paradigm of the learning organization is essentially that of stewardship of the vision, coaching and mentoring; not really traditional leadership from the front. This may, in fact, be entirely appropriate where we are talking purely of the rapid changes often necessary for normal or *ordinary* business development, which one could argue should largely accrue through competent ordinary management rather than extraordinary leadership.

Desirable a paradigm as this might be, I am afraid to say that all of my experience, over 20 years as a consultant in many countries and cultures where fundamental and usually cultural change is necessary for major organizational development, leads me to agree with John Kotter. My conclusion is that leaders – *extraordinary leaders* – if they do not actually have to 'drive' such changes through, particularly in the early stages, at least have to find leverage to energize this process. They have to role model their own conviction that the chosen picture of the future is preferable to the current reality, and demonstrate that they are comfortable with leading the journey from the front. They have to be prepared to introduce reward strategies and sanction those who are clearly not prepared to support or engage in the new work of pioneering the route. In crude terms, they have to get the message across that a fast-moving juggernaut is bearing down on people within a confined space and with little room for escape. People have two choices: to jump on board and enjoy the ride, or to be flattened. They can choose to be part of the team or not. I have no problem with the ethics of this provided that the vision and the strategies are ethically founded, the benefits communicated, and that those who do jump on board are rewarded (and I do not mean simply financially) for their loyalty, trust and support.

I have even met situations where one was forced to conclude that *in extremis* the end must sometimes justify the means. We know from history that this can be a high-risk and dangerous ideology for underpinning political strategy. It may, however, be necessary where a crisis has resulted not in the desirable sense of urgency being a catalyst, but in paralysis of thought and action that threatens to be terminal for the organization. It is, for example, usually perceived as more acceptable in extraordinary military situations requiring Special Forces operations. Here 'who dares wins' tactics can be, and often are, successful where the considered consensus is that ordinary or conventional approaches would not have been.

This too is an issue of communications. The difference, I suspect, is in the transparency. Special operations in the military sense are almost always covert. They have to be to retain the element of surprise and tactical advantage. Something equivalent to covert operations should necessarily be a part of new business development where security of corporate intelligence is paramount and industrial espionage rife. But any change programme that principally addresses fundamental and transformational organizational change as a whole must be transparent – even if it requires extraordinary daring and skills. The precise nature and gravity of the threat would not normally be made public in the former case, but it must be in the latter if people are to appreciate the urgency of the situation and the limited nature of the options. Preserving the status quo must be seen as an untenable option. I will deal later with the implications that this has for extraordinary leaders having to accept responsibility for containing anxiety and discomfort where not everyone in the organization is as sure as they (the leadership) may be of the outcome.

An interesting aside here is that in some countries it is now the law that workers must be consulted before major plans affecting them are put into effect. Marks & Spencer – the respected but troubled UK-based clothing and food retailer – found this out when its plans to close all of its overseas retail outlets were recently challenged in the courts in France because the employees had not been consulted in the process before the decision was announced.

5. Empowering broad-based action

Earlier I used a military analogy about the necessity to secure the ground before parachuting in with new weapons, tools and methodologies. In cases where paralysis of thought and action is the result of a total inability to address a crisis, it may be necessary to 'parachute in to secure the ground' in the first place, but this is an extreme scenario. In general I think it is fair to say that one important contributory reason for partial or total failure of the majority of major change programmes is that there is always a strong temptation to deploy the tactical elements and activities of the change programme too quickly. New concepts, re-engineering projects, departmental rationalization, and frequently external consultants, are routinely thrown into the fray before the organization – and that means the people – are properly prepared through careful development of their understanding of the situation and the threat posed by the status quo. The temptation is understandable. Projects, as we know, are always constrained by both budget and time, and we have recognized that there must be a sense of urgency. Furthermore there may be a disincentive to publicize proposals that could have an adverse effect on stock prices, even where employees should have a right to know.

This is a classic case of a dilemma where just the right amount of creative dynamic tension must be generated and then carefully controlled by the leadership. Not only do the big stones have to go in first; it must be seen that they cannot all be thrown in together, and the smaller stones have similarly to be trickled in carefully. Like watercolour painting, it requires a technique of 'more haste, less speed'.

Kotter points out the need to get rid of obstacles and change systems or structures that undermine the vision. Often such obstacles will be very 'big stones' that are, as it were, already stuck in the pot. Often it may be difficult to see how they can be removed without breaking the pot and occasionally this is the only answer, provided that the implications and process of making a new pot (or pots) to contain the new stones are fully understood. A less radical and less iconoclastic approach could be to try to break up the stones that are stuck, or re-arrange them. This will take longer but it will do less damage and there may be less chance of collateral damage and injury (physical or psychological) to bystanders.

Consultants often employ a force field analysis tool to help identify both the useful forces and influences, and the true nature of the impediments that exist in any dynamic situation where change is the challenge. The Mindworks Approach calls these 'bridges and barriers' and I will explore the process of identifying them and explain the way the analysis may be used to advantage in the next chapter. This model also advocates a methodology that I have found particularly useful where the 'gloom and doom' and the extent of the current problems – the adaptive challenge – may seem overwhelming and where it may be a cause of paralysis. Essentially this methodology involves forming a 'picture of the future' before attempting an exhaustive situational analysis of the 'current reality'. Not only does the picture of the future often prove inspirational, it can be generated without the danger of people becoming locked into current paradigms that are founded on existing mandates, structures or functions. The future appropriateness of these very tenets of the status quo can then be questioned when the current reality is considered.

The facilitation of systems thinking through the use of another tool in our Extraordinary Leadership Toolkit – the balanced scorecard Excellence Model – will help us to identify priorities for process improvement, and encourage non-traditional ideas for the empowerment of employees at all levels to take responsibility for the transformational activities that will be necessary. We will consider this in Chapter 7.

6. Generating quick wins

I believe that it is a sound strategy for the leadership in every change programme to facilitate the identification of potential 'quick wins' and to support and empower others to champion the process of their achievement. Once again Kotter is at pains to point out that change leaders must play a proactive role in this. You cannot just hope for quick wins: you have to create or generate them. This means that you have to plan for them. As we shall see later when addressing the issue of strategic and operational planning, it is quite normal for a rigorous situational analysis using the balanced scorecard model to generate around 150 Areas for Improvement, or AFIs, across all aspects of the organizational system. It may not even prove possible or credible to include all of these in a medium-term (say three- or five-year) plan. It will certainly be impossible to attempt to include more than a vital few in each annual operating (or business) plan, but it is advisable to try to ensure that results in one or two of these AFIs will constitute 'quick wins'. Potential impact against cost, and impact against the likely ease of implementation, are two possible analyses that can be conducted to facilitate the process of final selection of potential 'quick wins' that must then be project managed with appropriate resources and monitoring and evaluation of progress.

So much for planning and programming. Despite their importance, success will only be achieved through the commitment of good people on the ground and 'at the sharp end'. Neither the endorsement nor even the personal involvement of the leadership will be enough on their own to make new things happen. Ways must be found to reward and encourage those employees who do this. A good performance management system, which incorporates a performance review and appraisal system that is developmental as opposed to threatening, will prove helpful but is unlikely to be in place when quick wins are sought and achieved. Often this piece of the jigsaw, although a key to ultimate sustainability of the changes or reforms, will not be fitted until some way down the line. More immediate and probably creative ways must be found to recognize early contributions that add value and help to drive the process of change or reform. What is seen as appropriate recognition may be a factor of the prevailing culture of the organization or indeed of the new cultural paradigm that leaders are hoping to generate. Much has been written about reward strategies – both financial and non-financial – and I do not propose to explore the subject at length here.

We will consider the subject of best practice in performance management systems in Chapter 11. One thing is sure: the more organizations operate in the knowledge economy, the less they can afford to ignore their people on whose knowledge their future depends.

7. Consolidating gains and producing more change

There is no doubt that the laws of physics offer a number of interesting parallels when considering the leadership and management of change. I have always found that bearing Newton's Third Law in mind is useful when deciding what to do about the potentially helpful or constraining forces that are identified through force field analysis. This is hardly surprising given the model's genesis and its very use of the concept of forces.

Every action has an equal and opposite reaction. A blow with a hammer or even an axe on a particularly hard and resistant surface will result in the implement rebounding with almost equal force and perhaps even causing you injury. Applying the equivalent of brute force to intractable aspects of the status quo in organizations is equally likely to result in a strong and usually unhelpful reaction. On the other hand, if careful attention is given to subtly reducing or perhaps removing a number of lesser but nevertheless contributory resistances, and if a modicum of leadership and project management is applied to add weight to the positive side of the equation, the inertia and the friction can be reduced, and forward movement in the desired direction can result.

The increased credibility that results from the successful achievement of 'quick wins' can act similarly to reduce inertia and resistance, and add weight to the positive forces of change. This may be because people, when encouraged by demonstrable progress, are often more prepared to 'apply their shoulders to the wheel' and contribute the force of their efforts. When enough of them decide to do so, even solid and entrenched systems, structures and protocols will be seen to be built on sand after all. The same team strength that can then dismantle them relatively easily can be applied to replacing them with new systems, projects, themes and even new directions.

In the course of this process consideration should be given to hiring, promoting and developing those people who show that they can make it happen. They too will need to demonstrate extraordinary leadership at their respective levels of responsibility and authority and they will probably need to take risks and dare to win, knowing that their doing so is encouraged (within reason), and that it will bring rewards and appreciation.

8. Anchoring new approaches in the culture

I have said earlier that leaders now need to be able to hold the dynamic tension of a dilemma – that of managing performance and uncertainty at the same time. As a change programme moves through the eight stages that John Kotter has defined, and which I have illustrated, the uncertainty and anxiety should reduce as confidence grows. Nothing succeeds like success and this is particularly true where it is possible to articulate the connections between new behaviours and this success. Of course movement or progression through the stages will not be smooth or uninterrupted. It never is. It may prove necessary to regress deliberately to revisit and rework aspects of earlier stages that have proved to be incomplete or where it may be clear with the benefit of hindsight that apparent progress or achievement was illusory and is unlikely to be sustainable.

Good performance management will lead to greater productivity and improved customer relations and satisfaction. This will lend a higher degree of certainty to everyday operations and service delivery, but this too can be illusory as there is always more uncertainty out there. By the time that new approaches that are the product of a successful change programme are, as Kotter puts it, 'anchored' in the culture, it will normally be apparent that more change is necessary to remain competitive or to stay abreast of international standards of best practice. As this state of affairs – that is to say the need for continuous improvement – is now effectively a 'given' in fast-moving operating environments, it should be apparent that companies and organizations must build the capacity and the means for leadership development and succession.

The basis of this will be the empowerment of managers to extend their abilities and expand their competence. They can do this by taking responsibility for adaptive and generative work, and in so doing they can lay or build on a foundation for lifelong learning habits. They will need a framework and supportive systems to do this, however, and I will deal with these issues at greater length in Chapters 11and 12. If they have to keep looking elsewhere for new chief executives or other senior leaders it is a sure sign that many things are seriously wrong. One of them is the message that this sends out that either they failed to develop the next generation of leaders, or perhaps worse, they chose not to trust and back their judgement and place faith in the leadership potential of their loyal employees.

This phenomenon, which has become known as 'CEO churning' (a phrase coined by Bennis and O'Toole, 2000) seems to have become almost epidemic in its proportions. Commenting on it, *The Economist* recently pointed out that in February 2001, 119 CEOs left their jobs at sizeable American companies. This was 37 per cent more than in the same month a year earlier. Apparently departures in the last six months of 2000 were over 40 per cent up on the first six months of the year. This must point to a frightening and undoubtedly costly crisis of faith in companies' own ability to develop or 'grow' the leaders they need.

Boards (and ultimately shareholders) must be prepared to support the ultimately less expensive process of developing leadership competence at all levels. This is not to say that they should attempt to clone leaders to a preordained and currently fashionable pattern. Such a strategy would not be sustainable and such products could only ever be *ordinary* if they were allowed to 'mutate'. On the contrary, they should endeavour to sponsor frameworks of leadership competence development that will facilitate the building of a pool of talent that will always be large and diverse enough to produce leaders who can cope with extraordinary challenges at all levels. This should include more than one potential candidate for the top job at any given time in the company's future development. I will expand on the requirements for such a framework in Chapter 13.

6

The route plan

Everything should be made as simple as possible but not simpler.

Albert Einstein

ANALYSIS WITHOUT PARALYSIS

Senge (1990) points out that:

> *Creative tension cannot be generated from current reality alone. All the analysis in the world will never generate a vision. Many who are otherwise qualified to lead fail to do so because they try to substitute analysis for vision. . . What they never grasp is that the natural energy for changing (current) reality comes from holding a picture of what might be that is more important to people than what is.*

I have been fortunate to work and gain experience in a number of developing countries where the challenge is to improve the quality of service delivery and achieve better results against a backdrop of almost invariably severe financial constraints. In such situations it is often the case that managers have difficulty in 'seeing the wood for the trees'. They find it very hard to imagine a rosy future when everything around them (the current reality) spells gloom and doom, and they cannot imagine how proposals to challenge or change existing structures, functions or the status quo can hold out more than illusory promises. There is actually more to this than the pure difficulty of imagining a better situation. Psychologists use the term 'cognitive dissonance' to describe this phenomenon of seeing what we want to see – and therefore not seeing what we don't want to see. The phenomenon has been recognized for a very long time, as the Latin phrase *'Quod volimus credimus libenter'*, which means, 'We always believe what we want to believe', demonstrates.

This situation can often be prevalent in large, bloated and bureaucratic organizations or corporations where the 'led' become subject to cognitive dissonance through being under pressure to make out that things are going well even when they are not. Even when there is real awareness of the need for change, people may feel unable to challenge the way things have always been done. Protocols and processes may be wholly inappropriate and stultifying to corporate learning and only the brave or foolhardy will ever challenge the culture or put their heads above the parapet. How difficult it is in these circumstances, then, to be able to conceptualize, let alone engage in the adaptive work that is required to build a new more creative paradigm – one that will undoubtedly be necessary even to contemplate the potential opportunities of e-business.

Peter Senge and others are saying that creative tension is generated by the gap between a shared vision and a *clear* appreciation of the current situation. If one of these is missing there will be no useful creative tension. In such cases leaders need not only work to ensure that a shared vision is developed, they also need to be sure that they themselves, and everyone else, has a good grip on the current reality.

ANALYSIS, PLANNING AND ACTION

I am not going to suggest that anyone should substitute analysis for vision. In my experience there is actually a more common trap for the unwary. This is to substitute analysis for creative thinking or especially for action. In most change or reform programmes there is a tendency for management teams to find strategic planning rather seductive. It has a pleasing logic and it appears to distil order from chaos. The result, I am afraid to say, is usually a surfeit of strategic planning, very little strategic thinking, and virtually no strategic action. There is a tendency to try to produce the perfect plan – something that like the Holy Grail probably doesn't exist; or if it does will take an inordinate and unjustifiable amount of time and resources to find. Action without planning is, however, likely to be even more wasteful than planning without action. It was the doyen of management thinkers Peter Drucker who wrote: 'Plans are worthless, but planning is invaluable.'

The military draw a clear distinction between what they term 'an appreciation of the situation' and a 'plan' to deal with it. The appreciation is the analysis, and the physical distinction between two documents is quite useful, because it encourages decision making among options once thorough analysis has been conducted. The analysis serves not just to lay out all the facts available, but also to weigh the pros and cons of different alternative courses of action dispassionately. This tends to work very well at the level of individual tactical engagements where it is usually a straightforward matter to ask, 'Where are we now? What is our target destination? What are the different ways of getting there, and which appears to be the best way at this time and in the prevailing circumstances?'

All of these questions constitute the logic of the classical 'military appreciation'. (They also bear a close resemblance to the first steps of the Mindworks Approach that I shall outline in this chapter but there are important differences, as we shall see.) Once the decision is made – and it is facilitated by the risk analysis of the comparison of alternatives – the analytical appreciation can be left behind. It can be jettisoned like the booster stage of a rocket that has served its purpose and is now surplus to requirements.

The 'incrementalists' (Lindblom), and perhaps Mintzberg would probably argue that the classical appreciation is potentially flawed because it can lead to the dangerously delusive idea that one can be in control of the future and the inevitability of its emergence despite any strategy you try to create. They would not suggest, however, that strategy is not needed – rather that neither analysis nor planning constitute strategy and strategy must take account of the uncertainties. The Mindworks Approach does this.

Instinctive decision making

Actually the classical appreciation model, or at least its basic form, can prove very valuable as a 'quick and dirty' check on the gut feelings that leaders often have about the correct direction to move or decision to make. The instincts of exceptional leaders are more often than not right. This is partly what makes them extraordinary. Mant (1997) puts it rather nicely when he describes this instinctive process, calling it 'the anatomy of timely decision-making':

> *Effective Executives at full stretch, should be under time pressure. Good judgement means that a sound decision can be taken fast, before the solution is obvious. The decision works its way up from 'gut-feel' to an intellectual rationalization. It has usually reached about gullet level when the time comes for the decisive executive to decide.*

When such instinctive or unqualified decision making precedes and influences the outcome of rigorous analysis, reducing the latter to justification of the leader's preferred course of action, it is called 'situating the appreciation' and in such cases it is rightly to be disparaged.

Nevertheless, it is worth considering what lies behind intuition and instinct. Even though it may not be conscious thinking that Mant is describing here, it is probable that some 'thinking' is taking place. Let us consider the simplistic but useful concept that the left side of the brain deals with logic, symbols, time and so on, while the right side deals with images, connections, etc. What may be happening when people use their intuition is that there is some processing taking place in the right brain. It is linking together information and experience and, when it recognizes a pattern or fits a new piece of information into a bigger picture, it sends some form of recognition signal and guides the left brain to reach a conclusion or decision of some kind.

I have always believed that something similar happens when people with 'an aptitude' for learning foreign languages seem to be able to get the sense of a phrase even when it contains words they do not know, and fit it into the overall context. Most people would stop short at an unrecognized word and miss what follows. Such individuals seem to have the ability not only to let the unknown element pass in order to pick up the sense of the whole phrase, but then later to recall the unknown word and deduce its proper meaning. The brain says 'Aha – so that word must mean. . .' The final step to validation and retention of this newfound learning, which completes the feedback loop, is to play it back proactively by using it in a phrase. If it works the learning is valid and the future use of it is both logical and instinctive. The relatively intense concentration that this process requires (listening carefully and attempting rapidly to translate) in fact puts the brain under pressure, which may possibly speed up or facilitate this processing in the right brain in some way. Perhaps extraordinary leaders tend to have a ready facility to make such rapid connections between the known and the unknown and be right more often than not.

Where the situation and its challenges are more complex than the scenario of the individual tactical engagement, and especially where there is a requirement to plan for a scheduled or integrated programme of action to address many issues, there is, as Drucker says, no substitute for a planning process that includes some form of rigorous appreciation or situational analysis. How we get managers to turn the plans (which Drucker reminds us are 'worthless' in themselves) into action is another matter, and I shall attempt to throw some light on this later because it is fundamental to the 'worth' of the whole exercise.

THE MINDWORKS APPROACH

The Mindworks Approach was conceived by Andrew Cooper and Jane Landy from a UK and Ireland based consulting company called Mindworks in 1996. Its purpose is to provide people who want to change an organization, set up a new one, or to think about their future, with a straightforward way of doing the analytical and creative thinking which is necessary in any of these situations. It highlights nine steps to analyse and think about the necessity for change (as opposed to Kotter's eight stages of leading the process of implementation). Kotter's stages help you to think about the conditions necessary for successful implementation and the order of attempting to create them. They do not tell you what or how to change, or how to define this. The Mindworks Approach helps you to work out, from first principles, what your organization should be doing and whether it needs to change in order to do it better.

Change always requires some hard thinking. When thinking about one's own organization it can be difficult to stand back from the complex and frequently sensitive issues that arise when change is being considered. When developing a new organization or possibly a new Internet venture, it is particularly easy to get overwhelmed by the complexity of the task.

Andrew Cooper explains what they were aiming to do in developing the Mindworks Approach:

We wanted to develop an approach to thinking about organizations and change which was as simple as possible without being simplistic. The *nine-step process can be seen on one level as simple common sense. It provides a structure that helps people to address a series of straightforward who/what/how questions in a systematic way. One of the reasons for developing a simple process is that it needs to be (and is able to be) applied many times – in fact, continuously. We see it as an approach to management in general, rather than just a planning or change management technique. It is not just a linear process.*

I showed in Chapter 4 how it can be useful, and even therapeutic, to 'get up into the tower' and occasionally (or even regularly) gain an overview of the whole seemingly messy system. It is no good leaders doing this just for their own edification, even though it should clarify their own systems thinking. They must find ways to coach others to a holistic understanding of the systemic complexities and interdependencies, and then they must support, encourage and enable these people to develop new and innovative ways of dealing with the newly understood challenges. The leader's role as coach thus has two main components: to help the team to learn a new (but entirely common sense based) thinking process and technique, and then to help them to apply the product of the thinking to change their own situation.

Mindworks uses the word 'coach' to describe this helping role for three reasons. First, the term is more descriptive of the role that they have in mind here than the alternatives of 'internal consultant' or 'facilitator'. Second, most people will be familiar with the idea of a sports coach and can thus relate to the term more easily. Finally, there is increasing recognition of the role that leaders should play as coaches if they are able to. Not all have this ability, however: for example those who may be brilliant but erratic. Such individuals must surround themselves with good lieutenants who can act as a buffer to reduce the impact of the 'shocks' that their behaviour or ideas can cause, and who take on the responsibility for coaching the majority to an awareness of the potential value of seemingly crazy ideas.

While the ability to take on the role of coach is increasingly one that, as we shall see more than once in this book, is now highly desirable for all extraordinary leaders, it may be worth leaders considering the use of an independent coach for the purposes of this exercise. This will enable the leader or leaders of the management team themselves to take part in the strategic thinking analysis and in the process of arriving at consensus concerning conclusions as equal members of the team. The use of a coach who is experienced in the methodology will also help to increase the likelihood of high-quality results flowing from the process. Equally it should reduce the likelihood of this process getting bogged down in domestic issues, or being 'over-directed' by leaders who might be inclined to 'situate the appreciation' and skew the free flow of ideas.

Whoever you use to facilitate the particular process that we are considering here for 'coaching' the executive team through the necessary questioning and systems thinking, it may be worth bearing in mind that good coaching will always be based on some basic abilities that every effective (let alone extraordinary) leader must try to develop. These are:

I the ability to listen;

I the ability to clarify ideas;

I an understanding of coaching teams and mentoring individuals;

I a willingness to challenge ideas and to help people to ask (and answer) difficult questions;

I the ability to give useful and constructive feedback;

I patience;

I accessibility.

The background to the Mindworks Approach

Systems thinking underpins the whole of the Mindworks Approach. As we have already seen, systems thinking is a way of understanding the world in terms of the connections between things. One characteristic of this way of thinking is that complex things – including machines, organisms and organizations – can be examined at different 'levels'. For example, an internal combustion engine can be viewed in terms of the engine including parts of the various associated systems (electrical, fuel, etc) which are needed to make it function. It can also be viewed at the level of the specific sub-systems within the engine (such as the valve sub-system). Thinking in terms of hierarchies or levels helps to control the amount of complexity that is considered at any one time. Drawing a 'boundary' around a system enables the *interaction* between the system that is being considered (everything inside the boundary) and things that are in the environment of the system (everything outside the boundary which affects the system) to be examined. It is always difficult to try to be completely objective. You choose how you structure the hierarchy and where you place the boundaries of the various sub-systems depending on the particular purpose of your analysis.

The Excellence Model, which I will describe in detail in Chapter 8, incorporates nine components or 'sub-systems'. It is impossible to consider any one without reference to the others. Activities that appear at first glance to be firmly within the boundary of one of these components when viewed at one level (for example human resource management and development activities) will easily be seen to affect and impact on the others (for example customer or employee satisfaction). We shall see that these models both provide frameworks for helping management teams to formulate their picture of the future and their analysis of current reality. The use of the Excellence Model for these purposes can add value when it is used alongside the nine-step Mindworks Approach. The two methodologies are so complementary that together they can take you further than either was originally envisaged or expected to do in isolation. The Mindworks Approach, for example, was never intended to provide a comprehensive methodology for change and organizational design. Both models provide simple structures (or frameworks) for asking and answering some crucial questions in a way that ensures that the answers to one set of questions flows into the next.

The emphasis here is on both 'simple' and 'structured' because the nine steps are designed to be used by anyone in an organization (the CEO, the security section – anyone). It is useful to have a model that does not overburden people with complex or highly conceptual techniques and ideas. Andrew Cooper would say that one of the strengths of the nine steps is that they can be used with other techniques because they have been designed deliberately to enable this.

Later on in the planning process or cycle, both methodologies can be used again when going through the difficult step of trying to select the vital few priorities from what may be hundreds of areas for improvement, which will be identified when analysing the 'gap' or the journey from the present to the future.

The nine steps of the Mindworks Approach

The Mindworks Approach is divided into nine steps. The first five are essentially concerned with 'design' – developing a picture of the future essentially from first principles. The remaining four cover implementation. The steps are as follows:

1. *What* are you examining? (It could be the whole organization, part of it, a job, or even yourself!) Let us assume for our current purposes that it is the organization or business.

2. *Who* has needs that the organization could meet?

3. *What* needs does each group have which Step 1 could meet?

4. *How* can these needs be met?

5. *What* could the organization be like in the future? Which group's needs will it be meeting? How will it do that? What will it be like to work for? How will it deliver value?

6. *What* is the present situation – the current reality? What bridges (factors that could help) and what barriers (factors that could hinder) exist?

7. *How* could these bridges be exploited and barriers removed or overturned? What is the strength of their potential usefulness or the threat that they pose?

8. *Who* will do what, when and how to achieve the changes?

9. *Start* implementation and/or refine the above steps.

It is often useful when conducting Step 3 to consider and have the group or management team first produce a long list of 'whats' as they occur to them, and in no special order. Once this brainstorming and free flow of ideas has seemingly covered all the potential 'stakeholders' (a word Mindworks prefers not to use in order to keep the 'consultant-speak' to a minimum), they can normally be divided into groups with common principal interests. A shorter list of higher-level 'main whats' can then be distilled. Very often these will form the basis of the key results areas that will need to be captured later in the strategic plan.

The beauty of this simple approach is, of course, that it looks at the strategic thinking from the customer's or service user's perspective from the outset, and regardless of what the current mandate, structure or departmental functions imply or indicate. Furthermore, as I have said earlier, painting an impressionist picture of the future (that can later be refined) *before* describing the familiar (and often depressing or threatening) current reality, will normally prevent the team from getting bogged down in the apparent impossibility of the challenge of what may be perfectly possible, as well as necessary changes.

Table 6.1, on page 84, captures the nine steps of the Mindworks Approach and relates them to particular applications at various stages of the process of building a strategic plan.

I am grateful to Andrew Cooper of Mindworks for an artistic analogy: Leonardo Da Vinci didn't paint the Mona Lisa by starting in the top left-hand corner of his canvas and working slowly and methodically downwards until he finished in the bottom right-hand corner with a complex picture. He would have started with a general idea of what he wanted to achieve and then would have roughed out sketches – many of which were probably thrown away. Even while he was painting he would have changed the detail until he was eventually satisfied. The obvious difference between this analogy and planning for an organization is that in the latter case there never is any final fixed end result. The future stretches endlessly before us and our picture of it is continuously changing.

In conclusion let us consider further some of the ideas that underlie the nine steps:

▮ why organizations need to be designed;

▮ applying engineering principles to organizations;

▮ why organizations are messy and why they are difficult to design;

▮ links to evolution – of mankind, of ideas, and of organizations.

Organizations and design

We humans are pretty good at designing technologies – from flint arrowheads through to space shuttles - but we're not so hot at 'designing' organizations. This is partly because we don't think of organizations as requiring 'design', in the engineering sense. The tendency has always been to assemble enough of the right kinds of people together and lump them into appropriate divisions, provide them with a vision and mission, put some procedures and accounting systems in place and there you have it – a fully functioning organization. Clearly if we designed aircraft like this we would be in trouble – a Boeing 747 isn't the result of simply lumping together some wings, engines, a fuselage, flight controls and so on. The process starts with a well-defined overarching 'what' (the requirement being to transport x people y miles at no more than cost z and to do it as safely as possible time and time again). Everything that is present in the machine – the things that are the results of the designed 'hows' for this particular 'what' – are not only perfectly interconnected, they represent the minimum necessary set of interlinked components to achieve the design goals. The whole is, as Einstein suggested it should be, as simple as possible but no simpler!

If it is possible to design and configure a set of 'hows' for a specified 'what' in the engineering world, why can it be so very difficult when it comes to organizations? Undoubtedly the answer lies in the fact that people (who are the basis of all organizations) are, of course, neither machines nor parts of machines. We are not clones and each of us fortunately is unique. Mankind has evolved and evolution did not set out with an 'end' in mind.

Evolution

The 'what' – though unspecified – for evolution is to produce a self-replicating organism that is the 'best fit' for the environment in which it happens to exist. A common misconception regarding evolution is that humans (for example) are somehow 'better' than other species. In evolutionary terms, we're no better than ants (or any other currently existing species) and in some senses we're almost certainly 'worse'. There is a link here to the idea of 'memes'. Memes are 'units of cultural inheritance', eg stories, songs, ideas, and like genes they replicate and mutate. Returning to the responsibility of the leader for corporate learning, we could suggest that if a leader can create an organization in which memes can propagate and replicate effectively – with some copying errors to allow mutation – then he or she will have created an entity which does its own design work iteratively: changing itself to be the best fit for the circumstances in which it finds itself.

Table 6.1 *Strategic thinking – steps and outputs of the Mindworks Approach*

Step	Output	Immediate use	Future use	Documents used in
1. WHAT	Clarity on which organization or part of it is to be examined	Sets the scene for the scope of the analysis	Precedent for future consideration of other departments, acquisitions, etc	
2. WHO	Lists of customers, clients and other stakeholders who have needs to be met	Step 3a	Planning whom to consult	Summarized in situation analysis of plans, service delivery or partnering agreement
3a. WHATS	Long lists of required needs to be met	Step 3b	Marketing/product planning	
3b. MAIN WHATS	Shorter list of main 'results' or 'service areas'	Step 4	To derive the key results areas, strategic objectives, delivery strategies and performance measures	Strategic plan Business or operating plan Service delivery or partnering agreement
4. HOWS	Long lists of possible ways/ methods of addressing needs with alternatives	As background for Step 5	Delivery and business development strategies	Strategic plan
5. THE FUTURE	A clear picture or 'shared vision' of the desired future (in three to five years) (Which customers? Which hows? What image? What atmosphere?). A balanced scorecard like the Excellence Model can be used to help frame this picture	Defines the 'destination' of the transformation journey Step 6	Vision statement	Strategic plan

Step	Output	Immediate use	Future use	Documents used in
6. THE PRESENT	A clear understanding of the current reality. What 'bridges and barriers' exist? Lists of likely impediments to change and factors or influences that could help	Defines the 'starting point' of the journey. Step 7	Informs later base-lining workshop for a programme of self-assessment benchmarking	Strategic plan (challenges to be faced)
7. USING BRIDGES TO OVERCOME BARRIERS	How could bridges be exploited and barriers be removed?	Step 8	Informs priorities (Step 8) and later action planning for annual operational or business plan	Strategic plan (business or operating environment)
8. PLANNING AND PROGRAMMING THE CHANGE	Who will do what, when and how to achieve change? Detailed lists of activities with responsibilities and resources assigned	Evaluate and prioritize which actions to use in the transformation and define responsibilities and accountability. Step 9	To derive further change objectives and change strategies	Strategic plan Business plan
9. START IMPLEMENTATION	Achieving the transformation through adaptive work. Agreement, coaching, support and empowerment	'Quick wins'. Motivation through cause and effect connections	Performance improvement. Paradigm shift/new behaviours and organizational learning	Strategic and business plans. Benchmarking reports. 'Intellectual balance sheet'

The next chapter illustrates how best practice has developed over the last eight years to enable managers – and especially leaders – to take the systemic organizational overview when seeking the goal of continuous improvement of both design and results.

Part III

Converting vision into action

7

Launching into the future – checking the flight plan and the instrument panel

---

Effective leadership is not about making speeches or being liked; leadership is defined by results not attributes.

Peter F Drucker

MEASUREMENT AND MANAGEMENT

It is often said that 'if you can measure it you can manage it', and conversely, 'if it cannot be measured, it cannot be managed'. I have never thought that measurability is the most important criterion of management's ability to manage, but increasingly measurement has become a critical component of most good management systems. Most managers recognize its vital role in communicating performance indicators and targets, providing incentive through these challenges, and tracking the achievement of an organization's strategy through achievement of the operational objectives. Despite this recognition, however, most organizations do not operate with a measurement system that adequately fills all of these roles. Because conventional measures have mainly been financial indicators, most of today's measurement systems focus organizations on past performance and encourage a short-term view of strategy based on what are often knee-jerk reactions to six-monthly or annual financial profits and earnings statements. As such they often fail to provide the long-term strategic management capabilities that today's organizations and today's leaders need.

THE BALANCED SCORECARD – AN INSTRUMENT PANEL

We can compare financial turnover with distance travelled, but like this measure it is only one indicator. It is only one of the parameters needed to get a true picture of how you are doing, whether you are where you currently need to be on your journey, and whether there may be any warning indicators that might equate to fuel level, temperature or anything else. We will see that the balanced scorecard can act as an instrument panel that provides an overview of all of the necessary indicators and their relationships to one another. It provides the equivalent of readings of the balance sheet, the profit and loss account and the cash-flow forecast all at the same time; not just in the area of financial management or management accounting results and progress, but for the whole operating system in relation to its operating environment.

The balanced scorecard: a corporate global positioning system (GPS)

Two thousand two hundred years ago Sun Tzu, the Chinese military strategist and leadership 'guru', made several references in his famous treatise on *The Art of War* to the need for what we would now recognize as a balance of enabling criteria and results, or a balanced scorecard approach. For example he wrote:

> *Appraise your plans for competition using five basic factors. Assess yourself and compare your competitors to determine the best course. Consider everything. The five factors are: character, climate, structure, leadership, and information.*

In a reference to how one can destroy a competitor's reputation (and while pointing out that this is the least desirable and most dangerous competitive operation), Sun Tzu indicates that there are five areas that can be a focus for attacks on reputation. By inference we can construe that a good reputation may be built on these same five areas which, he said, are:

> *people or interpersonal relationships; organizational outputs or individual performance; customers or employees; suppliers or supporters; and capital resources or financial backing.*

There is, as they say, little new under the sun. No pun intended!

The balanced scorecard is a proven approach to strategic management that was originally conceived in order to embed long-term strategy into the management system through the mechanism of measurement. The balanced scorecard translates vision and strategy into a set of prioritized objectives that effectively communicate strategic intent and it motivates employees and tracks performance against the established goals. It has consequently become the foundation of a number of benchmarking systems to track both the degree and the rate of continuous improvement. Because of its holistic design concept it can, however, prove to be an excellent framework model for all improvement initiatives. The process of using it to 'score' performance, and the score itself, are actually secondary in importance to the understanding and insights that the model can generate for strategy formulation through the encouragement of systems thinking.

A vision describes the ultimate goal – to be the best, or as good as you can be if you operate in a non-competitive environment like the public services. A strategy is a shared understanding about how that goal is to be reached. The balanced scorecard normally provides a medium to translate the vision into a clear set of objectives for the improvement of current performance, and a coherent framework for combining and prioritizing them into a change strategy. These objectives are then further translated into a system of performance indicators and service delivery targets that effectively communicate a powerful, forward-looking, strategic focus to the entire organization and its customers and stakeholders. As such the scorecard can also be useful to senior management and executive teams in helping them to determine the scope and wording of the vision statement itself. Using it for this purpose will certainly help to ensure that the vision is grounded in practical and achievable strategic reality, and that it has an appropriately holistic ethos.

The four perspectives of progress

A well-equipped instrument panel will provide gauges for checking the 'levels' or the current performance state of a number of key indicators during the journey. In contrast to traditional, financially based measurement systems, the balanced scorecard solidifies an organization's focus on future success by setting objectives and measuring performance from four distinct perspectives which together give a balanced and holistic overview of organizational well-being. They are really the same for both private and public sectors. Good practice in most of these areas should have common denominators. Nevertheless, I have drawn out certain specific distinctions that may help leaders and managers from both camps to relate to the message.

The learning and growth perspective directs attention to the organization's principal asset and resource, and the basis of all future success – its people and infrastructure. Adequate investment in these areas is critical to all long-term success. The development of a true learning organization (and the responsibility for this is squarely one for the leadership) will significantly increase the job satisfaction of employees throughout the organization and this is one of the building blocks necessary to support success in the next balanced scorecard perspective: the internal perspective.

The internal perspective focuses attention on the performance or quality of the key internal processes that drive the business. Identification of processes that are key to performance improvement is an important leadership responsibility. The measurement of progress in implementation of continuous improvement strategies in these internal processes here and now is likely to be a key lead indicator of financial success in the future. However, in order to translate superior processes into financial success, companies must first satisfy, or preferably delight, their customers. There has to be a verifiable chain of cause and effect connections here that can justify investment in process improvement initiatives for customer satisfaction, and confirm the validity of the analysis and decision making that result from using the scorecard to help formulate strategy. Correct identification of critical processes and the decision to allocate resources to their improvement, must result in better-quality products or services that please customers, who spend more money and increase profits.

The customer's view of value for money is the ultimate arbiter of whether or not the product or service process is good enough.

Furthermore, full engagement of employees at all levels, seeking their ideas and views, and empowering them to take on adaptive work to make improvements in internal processes, has been found to be the key to success of any attempts to re-engineer processes. Business process improvement has, for the most part, replaced business process re-engineering, which often failed through its attempts to treat processes as if these were somehow unrelated to, and not dependent upon, the goodwill of customers and employees. Suppliers who also form part of the chain of key production processes are now seen correctly as partners with whom it is essential to foster the very best of relationships if continuous improvement in the 'harder' results criteria is sought.

The customer perspective ensures that we consider the business through the eyes of a customer, so that the organization retains a careful focus on customer needs and satisfaction. This can also take into consideration the impact on society as a whole, especially in the case of those businesses (and this will include most large and all multinational companies), that need to have ethical and responsible policies and strategies for environmental safety. Businesses must also assess the impact that their very size and influence have on local civil society, as a major employer and as a customer for other resources. Public sector organizations have a slightly different perspective on 'customers' and one that has developed significantly in the last decade through learning from effective best practice in the corporate arena. I will expand on this in the next section.

Finally, the *key performance results perspective* measures the ultimate results for which the business exists. These are usually the financial results that a corporate or commercial business provides to its share-holders, but this perspective can equally apply to other main results areas that the organization strives to achieve for its key stakeholders and partners. Examples could be brand image, maintenance of reputation for total quality of products and services, and so on.

Together, these four perspectives can provide a balanced view of both the present and future performance of the business or organization. When all four perspectives are considered together as a framework on which to hang an analysis of the management team's shared vision of the future, they go a long way to ensuring that strategy will be holistically coherent. Furthermore, there is a good chance that when the balanced scorecard is used rigorously by the executive team, the ultimate consensus about priorities for action, which is synthesized from the results of the various component analyses (from each perspective) will more than cancel out inevitable failure to agree on every detail, and that the exercise as a whole will thus add significant value to the strategic planning process.

The four perspectives of the public sector

Learning and growth. This perspective looks at the ability of public employees, the quality of information systems, and the effects of organizational alignment in supporting accomplishment of organizational goals for excellent service delivery. Processes will only succeed if adequately skilled and motivated public employees, supplied with accurate and timely information, are driving them. This perspective takes on increased importance in public service organizations that are undergoing radical change. Even learning to regard the public as valued clients or customers has necessitated a major paradigm shift in many countries and cultures, both at the national and local levels of service delivery. In order to meet these changing requirements and customer expectations, employees may be asked to take on dramatically new responsibilities, and may require skills, capabilities, technologies, and organizational designs that were not available before. Many senior civil servants did not even think of themselves as managers, let alone 'leaders' until quite recently.

Internal 'business' processes. This perspective focuses on the internal process results that lead to financial viability and satisfied customers just as it does in the private sector. To meet organizational objectives and customers' expectations, organizations must identify the key 'business' processes at which they must seek to excel. Key processes should then be (and now frequently are) monitored to ensure that outcomes will be satisfactory. Internal operational processes and the efficiency of their performance are the mechanisms through which the public's expectations concerning standards of service delivery are achieved. The problem often arises in civil and public services that the processes are perceived as being set in stone, only relevant internally, and not connected to customer convenience. This malaise is not, of course, confined to the public sector! In fact in the public sector they are often set in print in weighty volumes with archaic and bureaucratic systems for annual amendment, which may or may not take place. Ministerial or departmental mandates, protocols, regulatory frameworks and procedures, are frequently tied up in 'red tape'. This is usually just because they always have been, and employees have traditionally been expected to see these 'standard operating procedures' as somehow sacrosanct, rather than to question them or suggest improvements for greater efficiency or customer satisfaction. I recently came across rules in an Indian civil service manual that related to 'horse allowance', instructions for the required frequency of submission of expense claims to England via the Viceroy's office, and the existence of a post for a radio operator in each rural village which had been established in 1952 and never disestablished, with the result that they are still on the payroll!

Customer, client or user focus. This perspective captures the ability of the organization to provide quality standards of services, effectiveness of their delivery, and overall customer convenience and satisfaction. In the government or public service model, the principal driver of performance is different from that in the strictly commercial environment. Here customers and stakeholders take pre-eminence over financial results. This is not to say that financial prudence is not fundamentally important. In general, public organizations have a different, perhaps greater, stewardship, fiduciary responsibility and focus than do private sector entities. Responsibility for sound fiscal and expenditure management policy and strategies should, of course, be taken seriously by bureaucrats. The public (as share- or stockholders in this respect) expect it; but it should never be at the expense of the quality of the services that are provided within budgetary constraints.

Ensuring that policies, strategies and operations have a positive impact on society is, of course, more obviously a prime consideration for the public services whose very existence and raison d'etre is predicated on this. Finding metrics by which to measure this, and the trend over time, should, therefore, be a concern for leaders in all such organizations. Client Service (or Citizens') Charters have gone a long way to demystify the language of policy and to clarify just what government is offering its stakeholders and to what standard they have a right to expect the delivery of services. The balanced scorecard can be used effectively to benchmark these standards and enable political leaders to report honestly to the public on progress with policy intentions.

Financial. In the government arena, the 'financial' perspective therefore differs from that of the traditional private sector. Private sector financial objectives generally represent clear long-range targets for profit-seeking organizations operating in a purely commercial environment. Financial considerations for public service organizations have an enabling or a constraining role, but will rarely be the primary objective for 'business' systems. Success for public service organizations should be measured by how effectively and efficiently they meet the needs of their constituencies. Therefore, in the government arena, the financial perspective emphasizes cost efficiency, ie the ability to deliver maximum value to (and as perceived by) the customer.

RECOGNIZING A 'GOOD' BALANCED SCORECARD

The balanced scorecard has been quickly accepted by private and public sectors alike. It is easy to see the value to managers of a focused set of performance measurements that can tell them and their stakeholders or customers just how well they are doing. However, a more holistic and developmental view is that an effective balanced scorecard is more than a limited list of measures gathered into four or perhaps more categories. A good balanced scorecard should tell the story of your strategy or provide the framework for its development. Much well-documented practical application of the original theoretical model introduced by Kaplan and Norton (1992) in both the private and public sectors has now provided us with enough experience of best practice to be able to recognize the elements of a 'good' balanced scorecard. Three criteria help determine if the performance measures do, in fact, tell the story of your strategy:

1. *Cause and effect relationships.* Every measure selected for a balanced scorecard should be part of a chain of cause and effect relationships that represent the strategy.

2. *Performance drivers.* Measures common to most companies within an industry are known as 'lag indicators'. Examples include market share or customer retention. The drivers of performance ('lead indicators') tend to be unique because they reflect what is different about the strategy. A good balanced scorecard should have a mix of lead and lag indicators. Of course all measures will, by definition, be 'lagging' as they measure what has already happened. Some lower level lag indicators can be leading indicators for the higher level or strategic ones.

3. *Links to financials or key performance results.* With the proliferation of change programmes under way in most organizations today, it is easy to become preoccupied with specific goals such as quality, customer satisfaction or innovation. While these goals are frequently strategic, they must also track and translate into measures that are ultimately linked to financial viability indicators. We have

to identify the connections and suitable measures. If we can't do so, we can hardly use the model as a performance improvement tool.

Since initial publication in the *Harvard Business Review* the concept of the balanced scorecard has been interpreted in many different ways. While some people have chosen to view it simply as a focused set of financial and non-financial measures, there are dangers in such a simplistic interpretation. The measurement system may not reflect the strategy of the organization and too much concentration on the metrics can mistakenly guide an organization in directions that are not aligned with the strategy. This is one reason why I personally prefer to introduce management teams to the model initially as a framework for systems thinking during the planning process, rather than as a scoring or benchmarking tool. Once managers understand how useful and power-ful it is as a strategy development framework, they will be more inclined to ensure that when they do eventually attempt to agree baseline measures for their current performance, it will be with metrics that reflect a truly strategic performance improvement programme across the board of operations and relationships.

There needs to be an understanding of the 'flows' around a scorecard from box to box. To be effective it *must* be used to manage and not just to monitor. In the current climate this is what makes it difficult for companies (and perhaps the public sector as well) to justify returns on investment that are less rapid or dramatic in scale than the investors had hoped or expected. Nevertheless, many visionary firms do indeed outperform share price indices and always have done by engaging in long-term capability building, so it is naïve to suggest that markets simply do not allow companies and corporations to build for the future because of an all-pervasive short-term profits and earnings focus. Where they do this successfully, you can bet that there are committed people, and you can bet that they are committed because of extraordinary leadership!

One of the reasons that the leadership probably is extraordinary in such examples is that it is easy to manage by the scorecard in relatively benign times; but when the going gets tough, it takes leaders with *real and extraordinary commitment* and belief not to fly back to the financial box and do whatever is necessary to keep those results good in the short term. It can help if the overall performance reward framework can be linked into all stakeholders in the scorecard (not just shareholder value, although using the card should drive through to better results here too). Such mechanisms as share buy-backs may help manipulate this balance in the short term when necessary.

THE ART OF BUILDING A BALANCED SCORECARD

'Building a balanced scorecard seems simple, but is deceptively challenging.' This quote summarizes the frustrations of one executive who had embarked upon the development of a balanced scorecard with disappointing results. The design of a balanced scorecard should not be underestimated. If you really do wish to build a tailor-made one for your organization, as opposed to adopting and perhaps adapting one of the well-proven 'generic' models, there are two essential ingredients or requirements for successful bespoke design: an architect who has a clear vision, framework, philosophy, and a methodology for designing and developing the new management system; and a client who will be totally engaged and assume ultimate ownership of the project, understanding that they must live with the results long after the architect gives them the responsibility for managing them.

The client in this analogy is the executive team of the business or organization. Consultants who are specialists in benchmarking systems will often play the role of catalysts to the process, but the architect should really be the leadership of the business or organization. The balanced scorecard and the management system that will be built around it are ultimately the responsibility of the CEO and the executive team. Without their active sponsorship and participation, a balanced scorecard project should not be attempted, because it is doomed to failure. They represent what John Kotter calls 'the guiding coalition'. They may even use the scorecard to help them frame their vision and a holistic strategy for its achievement, but they must, in the process, become passionate about the improvement or change process, and they must have a sense of urgency in actively communicating their commitment to it.

A short case study – Executive Agencies in Tanzania

I arrived in Tanzania in early 1999 for a World Bank assignment as Performance Management Systems Adviser to the Government's Public Service Reform Programme. Shortly after my arrival I was asked by another adviser how I felt that we might address a problem which would not be common in the developed world but which I have found to be very common in developing and transitional countries undergoing major change and reform. A number of Executive Agencies had just been created to operate at arm's length from government – in fact with semi-autonomy in an 'eyes-on but hands-off relationship' with their parent ministries. Examples were the Civil Aviation Authority, The Airports Authority, The Roads Authority, The Meteorological Office and The National Bureau of Statistics. There was a real and genuine intention to try to map or baseline customer satisfaction with existing levels and standards of service delivery, and external consultants had been contracted to conduct customer satisfaction surveys across a wide geographical area at some considerable expense. The reports soon revealed that there was an extremely low level of awareness among the public about the standards that they had a right to expect, and a gloomy and cynical view about whether anything they said would make any difference anyway in an environment where resources were scarce but corruption was not. Consequently the consultants found it almost impossible to identify and propose realistic and suitable performance indicators or service delivery targets where none had previously existed.

The baseline performance surveys conducted by the consultants seemed essentially comprehensive and rigorous in their approach. The methodologies used, the decisions about what should be measured, and the priorities identified appeared sound. In fact a balanced score-card approach was actually used to good effect in one study done for The National Bureau of Statistics. The studies fell short of what was required in one major respect, however. They seemed to allow the Agencies 'off the hook' in relation to the fundamental need to define just how bad their past or current performance might be in some areas where, as a result, they decided not to select metrics. It is true that past performance may be difficult to measure in some cases where data have never been collected previously. It is probably also true that it may be perceived as threatening to some individuals who might feel that the exercise could be attempting to pin down what might be construed as blame for this state of affairs.

It is nevertheless fundamental to any process of strategic planning or benchmarking to be able to decide where you are now, and where you are trying to get to. This is basic navigation. It is of little use to either the crew or the passengers if the captain of a ship or plane knows where he wants to go but does not know where he currently is. Knowing that you are in difficulties is not enough either, if you are not sure where to direct the rescue services!

The first conclusion was, therefore, that perhaps the Agency teams should revisit the subject and try harder to identify just how they knew that there were weaknesses in some areas, and threats to the organization's future if these were not addressed. Was it complaints from customers – even if they had not been recorded? Was it evidence of business lost to competitors? Was it systemic, structural or bureaucratic obstacles that may be features of the current paradigm, which were going to impede them in taking advantage of their new-found freedom, but which could possibly be identified and removed? The first two could well be symptoms of the third. One study made a better attempt at addressing these issues than did the others and so it seemed that, on the face if it, there was no good reason why similar attempts could not be made to map customer satisfaction (for example) in the other Agencies.

We concluded initially that it should be possible for consultants to use the same approach to assisting the other Agencies to arrive at satisfaction indices. In order to keep it simple we decided that it was a question of focusing on the 'vital three' results areas of customer satisfaction, flexibility/responsiveness (which can be both external and internal), and productivity (which is essentially concerned with internal measures, including financial ones, and should therefore be capable of being measured more easily). In the context of this last criterion, we felt that management might find it helpful to try to map the competencies which existing accounts staff had in order to identify any gaps between current levels and those which would evidence progress towards known best practice.

STANDARDS

In addition to using this simple balanced scorecard methodology, it might be helpful to think in terms of standards. What standards of service delivery do customers expect? What standards do competitors demonstrate; and can we identify the standards to which people currently perform vis-à-vis accepted best practice?. Indicators for these standards will tend, in the main, to fall into these same three groups:

1. those concerned with customer satisfaction;

2. those concerned with flexibility and responsiveness;

3. those concerned with productivity (efficiency and effectiveness).

High standards of performance in the second and third areas obviously help to generate the customer satisfaction which we would like the first group of indicators to evidence. In all three cases they will encompass the need (as priorities dictate at any given time) to manage activities, resources, people, and information at the operational level.

If data are currently missing to help you assess just how bad you are at doing this, ensuring the future availability of more and better data should itself be a priority for improvement of either individual staff competencies for its collection, or management information systems (MIS), or probably both. This statement introduces another potential paradox about how we measure or map competence and what exactly it is. Competencies are a combination of underpinning theoretical knowledge and practical experience which together result in the skills required to carry out elements of one's work or job to a satisfactory (or better still – a high) standard, as benchmarked by internationally recognized good practice in any particular field. We may have insufficient data about current customer satisfaction but there is a wealth of good material available concerning management standards and definitions of the competencies needed for best-practice performance to internationally benchmarked standards. Using these guidelines we can assess our current competencies (eg for the management team's management of activities, resources, people and information) and thus determine what we have to do to improve our competence to deliver higher standards of service in future. Management teams should not worry about definitions of the standards at this point. Necessary materials and facilitation of training in their use are readily available from consultants that specialize in acting as catalysts to the process, and it is also quite possible to undertake self-assessment using published and well-proven guidelines.

A CORPORATE POSITIONAL FIX

So what can you do if you wish to consider such an approach? The following is a suggested 10-point checklist for conducting a navigational fix on your current corporate position:

1. Map current competence profiles of teams and individuals by using a self-assessment methodology against benchmark international standards. (The EFQM Excellence Model described in Chapter 8 can be used for this process.)

2. Attempt to map competitors' current competence in the same way and against the same benchmark standards.

3. Identify HRD and corporate learning priorities in line with potential areas for competitive advantage.

4. Develop MIS to gather better data in future about customer (and perhaps employee) satisfaction. This will help keep a check on the appropriateness of the perceived required competencies.

5. Make and communicate plans to attend to 'hygiene factors' as soon as possible. These are those basic issues like quality of the working environment, the basic wage, health and safety at work, etc, which, if not dealt with, will continue to have an adverse (or at worst paralysing) effect on employees' morale and motivation. There is no point in even considering more sophisticated mechanisms for motivation (like performance-related pay systems) if the basics are not right. Abolish outdated and bureaucratic systems and structures that impede results-oriented ways of working.

6. Plan 'motivator factors' for the future when efficiency savings (or even just a better climate for improved communications between management and staff at all levels) could offer opportunities to reward those who make 'wins' possible. When attempting to identify and recognize such individuals we should always remember that while a few people may have performed conspicuously well, they will almost certainly have been supported by a majority of employees who just go to work and get on with the job to the best of their ability, generally doing a very competent job. Without them the organization would probably grind to a halt, but they often don't receive or expect much recognition. The deliberate identification of team targets and the recognition and reward of team success can be the answer to this, with personal mentions that cost nothing but mean so much to those concerned.

7. Communicate the vision, mission and strategic objectives constantly so that nobody is in any doubt about how individual performance targets track directly and logically to the 'vital three' corporate key result areas of customer satisfaction, flexibility/ responsiveness, and improved productivity.

8.   Make all team and individual output targets as SMART as possible.

9.   Compare rates of improvement, not only against plans (or as simple statistical increases or decreases), but also against competitors' progress and customers' expectations, which will inevitably grow as the 'market' becomes more sophisticated.

10.   In summary: implement the following diagnosis and improvement model:

- Become aware (and coach everyone to become aware) of 'gaps' between current and desired _standards_ of service delivery. Required standards should, of course, be based on stakeholder needs.

- Identify the nature and seriousness of these 'gaps'.

- Identify possible causes – both system-related and employee-competence-related. A word of caution is, however, necessary here. It is important to identify cases of inadequate competence but just as important not to jump to apportion blame! In most cases it will be due to a system/management/organizational problem, and no reason to sack the workers! If employee competencies are in question, it is certain that the HR processes for establishing needs for job and person specifications, recruitment, training and development, appraisal, and so on, should also be questioned. Deming reminded us that 85 per cent of problems are caused by management, not workers!

- Develop action plans to reduce impediments and resistances.

- Implement the action plans.

- Evaluate improvements by self-assessment and external independent assessment if possible. Have they solved the problems?

- Review the new state of affairs (eg the rate of improvement against customers' expectations and competitors' progress).

Such lists are easy to write and difficult to execute! I will endeavour to describe later (in Chapters 11 and 12) what the new performance paradigm could look like and how it must derive directly and logically from the organization's strategic plan. Note particularly how all operations must track both directly (vertically) to key result areas or strategic objectives through strategies and business processes which are central to the performance improvement effort (ie customer satisfaction, flexibility/responsiveness, and productivity), but also holistically (ie horizontally) to each other. This will ensure that the features of such a new excellence paradigm are that it:

▮ is externally focused;

▮ is internally focused (at the same time);

▮ has integrated processes;

▮ reflects global best practice and competitive awareness;

▮ frames the systems thinking approach to performance management;

▮ points to the need to address assessment of individual and team competence to achieve planned improvement targets. This is also a check on how realistic targets are in a given time frame.

APPLYING A PROVEN METHODOLOGY

While it is perfectly possible to design your own bespoke scorecard, I believe that you will save yourself a lot of heartache and sleepless nights by adopting and perhaps adapting a tried and tested methodology as we did in the example summarized in the case study. This approach will usually ensure the capture (and translation to measurement when required) of an organizational strategy across a wide variety of strategic and operational situations. In any event you need to consider at this point whether you wish to use the balanced scorecard alone as your principal model to develop overall strategy (to be captured in a strategic or business plan). You may prefer to use the scorecard to ensure a comprehensive and holistic systems view, and to identify areas for improvement when using another model such as the Mindworks Approach to formulate the main strategic objectives. In either case it is possible to use the scorecard regularly thereafter (perhaps at six-monthly or annual intervals depending on the pace of change) for actual 'scoring' or benchmarking of continuous performance improvements in all chosen perspectives once you have determined the priorities for attention and action planning.

Arguably balanced scorecards should be used more frequently for monitoring and managing operational measures, especially with the role of translating strategy into action. This will avoid the situation where the management team look at the financials on a daily, weekly and monthly basis, but consign the non-financials to an occasional check.

Some consulting firms specialize in providing a service to senior managers and business leaders as architects of the measurement system. US consulting firm Renaissance Consulting employ a four-phased approach in designing a bespoke balanced scorecard measurement system for clients. The generic framework for this is available on the World Wide Web and I am grateful to Renaissance for permission to reproduce it here.

Step 1: Define the measurement architecture

Because the balanced scorecard should reflect the strategy, an organization must develop a *distinct* strategy. A business strategy and a balanced scorecard that describes it are not random. Renaissance have found that the architecture of a balanced scorecard has several dimensions that must be incorporated into scorecard design. A good design process will recognize these dimensions and provide frameworks to guide the architect and the executive team in their thinking about the strategy. There are frameworks that describe the strategy and represent the foundation on which a complex design is based. For example, in the financial perspective, one could frame discussions about the three primary components of a financial strategy: (1) revenue growth/mix, (2) productivity, and (3) asset utilization. Whether operating a growing, mature, or harvest-oriented business, executive teams use this framework to anchor their financial objectives. Similar frameworks for the customer, internal, and learning perspectives give both the architect and clients a common ground from which to consider the setting of strategic objectives.

Step 2: Build consensus around strategic objectives

It is common and normal for a management team not to share full consensus on the relative importance of its strategic objectives. Even harmonious management groups in well-managed organizations will often lack a shared understanding about the overall strategy and the relative roles of different groups within the organization, and this can keep the team from agreeing on priorities. The second step of the development process is designed to build consensus among the members of the executive team around the long-term strategic priorities of the organization. To achieve this goal, each executive team member is interviewed individually by Renaissance consultants to capture his or her implicit and explicit strategies for the business. These personal visions are then synthesized into feedback that is reviewed at an executive workshop. During this session, the executive team learn about where there is and is not consensus about their strategy and discuss unresolved issues. Ultimately, a coherent group vision for the organization emerges in the form of 10 top priority objectives.

Step 3: Select and design measures

With the prioritized strategic objectives agreed upon by the executive team, the next step is the selection of measures to track the achievement of these objectives. Sub-team working sessions focus on the development of measures for a subset of the objectives, finalizing the wording of objectives and searching for measures appropriate for tracking each objective. At the end of this step, the sub-teams synthesize their recommendations into a united 'strategic story.' With agreement on the strategic objectives and measures, the balanced scorecard measurement system design is complete.

Step 4: Develop the implementation plan

For a balanced scorecard measurement system to create value, it must be integrated into the management system of the organization. The final step of the process entails three primary tasks: (1) identifying the current practices in various management processes, (2) evaluating opportunities for integrating the balanced scorecard into the management process, and (3) developing an implementation plan. This step typically reviews the client's approach to data reporting and review, management meetings and decision making, strategic learning, strategic communication, personal objective setting and planning and budgeting.

UNLOCKING THE STRATEGIC PAY-OFF

Companies that have been using the balanced scorecard for some time and have successfully integrated the tool into their management processes are beginning to see significant financial and operational results. The CEO of a large insurance company estimates that by using their scorecard as a catalyst for MIS improvements, he was able to increase product profitability by nearly $30 million over a two-year period. Others describe the intangible benefits gained from being able to 'understand the drivers of business success' and 'educate the organization, deciding how, when and where to raise the bar'.

By developing a balanced scorecard that truly tells the story of your strategy, you will set the foundation for a management system that is capable of driving dramatic improvements in performance.

8

Leading excellence

A leader leads the organization up the ladder of expectations, and when the time is right, kicks away the ladder.

Sun Tzu

THE EFQM EXCELLENCE MODEL

A ready-made generic balanced scorecard methodology that has gained very considerable currency throughout Europe in both public and private sectors is the European Foundation for Quality Management's Excellence Model. Lessons from the UK government's Public Sector Benchmarking Project over a period of seven years have now led to very significant and measurable improvements in service delivery standards in public services. Monitoring and evaluation of the project over this period has produced modifications and improvements in the latest version of the model.

In fact, in less than 10 years, the principles of business excellence have permeated organizational life from one end of Europe to the other, and from the largest global enterprises, major parts of government, public sector agencies, healthcare, schools, police authorities, to the research laboratory, the professions, and small businesses. To have this appeal, the underlying principles of the EFQM Excellence Model must reflect widely held views on best organizational practice, including continuous learning, improvement and innovation. Leaders will find that in this they have a really practical balanced framework for all improvement initiatives in pursuit of their vision and their plans for 'what might be'. It should prove particularly helpful in the new context of analysing how e-issues may now have to permeate all aspects of an organization that seriously intends to remain competitive.

The Excellence Model is useful in conjunction with Steps 5 and 6 of the Mindworks Approach to help management teams frame a picture of what the future might be like and then establishing the 'gap' between this and the current situation. Focus can be achieved through framing the analysis in terms of the model's nine criteria (see Figure 8.1), which are:

1. leadership;

2. policy and strategy;

3. people (human resource management);

4. partnerships and resources;

5. processes;

6. customer results (satisfaction);

7. people results (employee satisfaction);

8. society results (impact on the wider community);

9. key performance results.

The first five of these are known as 'enabler criteria'. The others are the 'results criteria'. All are interdependent in so far as any activity in any criterion area will impact on all of the others to some degree. It should go without saying that the quality and quantity of leadership inputs and influence will have significant effects and impact, not only on the various results areas but also in all of the other enabler criteria. For organizations that are interested in benchmarking their performance improvement there is an internationally accepted scoring system for

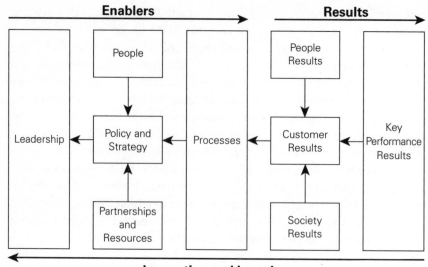

Figure 8.1 *The EFQM Excellence Model*

the model and it is even possible to have external assessment for award-level organizational excellence. When the model is used to actually score current performance and/or to benchmark it against previous scores or those of other similar organizations, each criterion is given a weighting to reflect its perceived relative importance to the others. I have omitted these weightings and details of the scoring methodology in this description because I want to underline the model's usefulness as a framework for strategy formulation and for determining priorities for improvements across the board. For those who wish to know more about this, or to seek help with it, reference to appropriate Web sites is made in the Acknowledgements at the front of this book.

A word of caution about priorities may, however, be necessary. Priorities for improvement (even in organizational design) can and should be defined continuously. Priorities in design, perhaps when establishing a new venture or organization, are more difficult to define. It would be crazy, for example, to try to decide when designing an aircraft to a budget (an engineered and mechanical object and yet a complex amalgam of interdependent systems if ever there was one), which was more important – the engine, the wings, the fuselage or the instruments. Clearly they are all equally 'important'. The true priorities here become those pertaining to greater efficiency, greater safety, or perhaps cost-effectiveness. Experience is as important as innovation.

LEADERSHIP – THE FUNDAMENTAL ENABLER

This criterion deals with how leaders develop and facilitate the achievement of the mission and vision, how they develop values required for long-term success and implement these via appropriate actions and behaviours. It also seeks to question the extent to which leaders are personally involved in ensuring that the organization's management system is developed and implemented.

The criterion draws attention to the actual behaviour of leaders in reinforcing the agreed values and expectations in order to develop and reinforce the organizational purpose, direction and culture of excellence. This implies a requirement to role model expected behaviour, but also to be held accountable and, in effect, to be measured on their effectiveness in doing this. Do leaders get personally involved, for example, in training and development activities? How extensive is their involvement?

I am indebted to BQC Performance Management Ltd, one of the consulting companies contracted by the UK government's Cabinet Office for the UK Public Sector Benchmarking Project, for permission to reproduce the following sets of questions from Bratt and Gallacher (1988). These questions prompt rigorous thinking by the executive or management team in the process of using the Excellence Model to develop strategy and seek areas for improvement in performance. Similar sets of prompts are available for each of the other criteria, which are all, of course, as we have seen, interdependent. It should be clear that leadership has, or should have, a significant impact on policy and strategy formulation, on people and their management through HRD and HRM practices, on resources and partnerships and, of course, on the identification and improvement of key processes. For now we will concentrate just on the sort of questions that the leadership should ask concerning its own fitness for role. Their comprehensive nature will, I trust, give a flavour of the very thorough analysis of the whole organizational system that a complete self-assessment exercise can provide.

Prompts for the leadership criterion

The following sets of questions will prompt you and your management team to consider:

- *how leaders develop and facilitate the achievement of the mission and vision;*

> – *how they develop values required for long-term success and implement these via actions and behaviours;*
> – *how they are personally involved in ensuring that the organization's management system is developed and implemented.*

NB: The term 'leader' is used in this criterion to include everyone who has staff reporting to them at any level in the organization.

Leaders develop the mission, vision and values and are role models of a culture of excellence

▌ How are leaders involved in establishing the mission, vision and values and the behaviours expected in the organization?

▌ Does the actual behaviour of leaders reinforce the values, behaviour and expectations set by the organization?

▌ How are leaders held accountable for, and measured, on their role model behaviour?

▌ Do leaders get involved in giving training? How many leaders are involved? How extensive is their involvement?

▌ Do they personally get involved in improvement activities? Is this involvement visible outside their department?

▌ Do leaders set aside time and resource for facilitation activities? Do leaders facilitate improvement activity themselves rather than use specialists?

▌ Are leaders involved and visible in activities such as goal-setting, prioritizing improvements, and reviewing improvement performance?

▌ Are the budgets for improvement activity devolved down through the management levels? Do leaders make full use of their improvement budgets?

▌ How do leaders balance the pressure of meeting operational targets and allowing their staff to get involved in improvement activity?

▌ How do leaders plan to stimulate innovation and creativity and empower their people?

▎ How do leaders focus on the importance of learning?

▎ How do leaders emphasize the importance of cooperation across the organization?

▎ How do they gather feedback to review their leadership style and use it to improve (for example through 360 degree appraisal)?

Leaders are personally involved in ensuring the organization's management system is developed, implemented and continuously improved

▎ Have leaders identified competencies in improvement and used them in staff development?

▎ How is the organization structured to deliver the strategy developed by its leaders?

▎ How is process management systematically used?

▎ Is there clear ownership of processes across the management structure of the organization?

▎ How do leaders put in place a system for developing, implementing and updating the organization's strategy?

▎ How do leaders put in place a system for focusing on the key results indicating the success of the strategy?

▎ How do leaders establish a process to implement their plan to stimulate innovation and creativity in their people?

▎ What cross-section of leaders is involved in reviewing and improving the management systems?

Leaders are involved with customers, partners and representatives of society

▎ How do leaders prioritize their activities with different customer groups?

▌ Is there a strategy of partnering with key customers, and are leaders involved in leading these activities?

▌ Is there a strategy of partnering with other organizations, eg joint ventures, and are leaders involved in leading these activities?

▌ Is this involvement broadly spread, or is it restricted to those for whom it is an integral part of the job, for example sales and marketing leaders meeting customers, and purchasing leaders meeting suppliers?

▌ Do these contacts address joint improvement and partnership issues or are they mainly fire-fighting/progress-chasing sessions?

▌ Are these contacts geared to identifying future needs before they become an issue (ie prevention based) or do they only address requirements already found to be needed?

▌ Do you have a policy, or other guidance, on your involvement in promoting business excellence outside the organization?

▌ What range of leaders has been involved in promoting business excellence outside your unit by, for example:

– giving talks/training to other units within the organization;

– giving talks to professional bodies, local organizations and/or conferences;

– giving talks/training to suppliers or customers;

– leading cross-organizational teams, for example looking at best practice;

– writing articles for external publications?

▌ Are leaders' memberships of professional bodies helpful in actively promoting business excellence?

▌ How are leaders directly involved in corporate citizenship activities?

▌ Are these external activities integrated into the normal management process, or are they an unconnected sideline?

▌ Is recognition for excellence and continuous improvement also provided outside the organization, for example to customers, suppliers and other external stakeholders?

Leaders motivate, support and recognize the organization's people

▌ How do leaders deliberately make themselves accessible to their staff?

▌ How do they communicate with their staff? Do they make specific opportunities to listen to their staff?

▌ How do leaders clearly communicate where the organization is going and how their people can contribute?

▌ How do leaders support their people in making that contribution?

▌ How do leaders emphasize the importance of improvement activity and make it possible for their people to get involved?

▌ Do leaders expect or require commitment to, and involvement in, improvement activities when appraising their staff?

▌ Is there a clear link between commitment to, and involvement in, improvement activities, and the criteria leaders use to select staff for promotion?

▌ What processes exist to involve leaders in recognizing individuals and teams for outstanding performance? How do leaders get involved personally with this recognition?

▌ Is the performance of teams and individuals in excellence and continuous improvement recognized and rewarded at the same level as other business considerations, for example in comparison with any personal productivity objectives and bonus schemes?

▌ What is the relative emphasis placed on team recognition versus individual recognition? Does it support any value relating to team-work?

▌ Do all leaders give recognition, or is it the same few all the time? (Is there an underlying approach or is it left to individual leaders?)

▌ Have leaders been given any guidance and/or training on how to give recognition?

I think we would all agree that to find leaders who really do manage to do all of these admirable things in an organization that facilitates this paradigm would indeed be extraordinary. These are obviously descriptions of a 'perfect world', but they are drawn not just from theory but from internationally recognized best practice. In the overall scoring system for the model when it is used for benchmarking, it is recognized that a score of 50 per cent is a very good score. It usually takes a business seven years to become a true total quality organization and it would not be unrealistic to suggest that reaching an award-level score in the 75 per cent range would also take a similar amount of time and hard work. In this perspective perhaps even the extraordinary challenge for leaders becomes potentially possible.

As Peter Senge says, analysis can be no substitute for vision, but it can help to frame people's thinking about what they would otherwise find difficult to envisage. I have advocated doing this rigorous analysis initially in order to colour in a 'picture of the future' where in the medium term (say five years) it is probably reasonable to aspire to achievement of quite a lot of what is described above as 'excellent' leadership behaviour. Ask yourself just how competitive your business will be in five years' time if you cannot imagine it displaying such standards! It is then necessary to go through the same analysis to produce a comprehensive picture of the organization's present operating environment, and its current standards of performance and service delivery. Comparison of the two states reveals the performance 'gap' that has to be bridged – and indicates the degree of difficulty that can be anticipated on the 'journey'. I suggest that such a process would be particularly useful for senior management of a 'conventional' or 'traditional' business attempting to envisage the scale of the challenges for funding, organizing and *leading* the implementation of an e-strategy.

Frequently a list of 100 to 150 areas for improvement (or perhaps radical change) will emerge from this analysis for all nine criteria – say around 15 per criterion. These (or at least a prioritized 'vital few' of them) must be factored into the key results areas and strategic objectives, which will normally have been derived (or will subsequently be derived) from the Mindworks strategic thinking exercise or some other methodology for producing a strategic plan. A full description of a suggested comprehensive process for facilitating the strategic and business planning process will follow in Chapter 10.

USING RADAR TO NAVIGATE

(RADAR is a registered trademark of EFQM.)

In parallel with the launch of the improved Excellence Model in 1999, the EFQM also introduced the RADAR concept of scoring for use when benchmarking performance improvements (through self-assessment as part of an internal performance management system, or external assessment for awards). Whether or not management teams are interested in actually assessing or scoring their results and service delivery improvements in this way, this enhancement of the model is useful for leaders to monitor and evaluate their organization's progress as a 'learning organization'.

The guidelines provided by EFQM and by the UK government's Cabinet Office (in the context of public sector benchmarking projects) give useful pointers to and descriptions of what is widely considered to be international best practice in exemplary or 'star' organizations. As such – just like the stars themselves – these pointers are useful for 'navigation'.

The principle is that an organization needs to:

▮ Be clear about the *results* it is to achieve if it is successfully to meet the expectations of its customers and stakeholders such as employees and the wider community. Consideration and analysis of results can cover trends, targets, comparisons, causes and scope. Expectations and numbers of potential e-customers identified from technographics research (perhaps with huge implications for exponential growth and global market penetration) must also be considered here.

▮ Put *approaches* in place that will drive towards those results, bearing in mind all of the resulting effects to the balance of other enabler criteria, particularly resources. Approaches have to be both sound (proven to produce improvements) and integrated (with others for other criteria).

▍ Ensure that *deployment* of these approaches is effectively and extensively implemented in a structured and systematic way despite the probable need for a sense of urgency.

▍ *Assess and review* how effective these approaches and their deployment are in the continuing drive towards the desired results. The cycle for such monitoring and evaluation may well have to become shorter and shorter as rapid e-business growth displaces traditional sales or marketing operations in many organizations. Effectiveness in this context is a factor of measurement, learning and improvement. An assessment against the model is rather like a rigorous annual mechanical safety check on a car (like the UK's Ministry of Transport test) to see if all is fundamentally safe and sound. The scorecard is more like the instrument panel, as we have seen.

This new augmentation of the original methodology is of particular interest to business or organizational leaders who recognize the value of innovation and organizational learning. Making cause and effect connections and learning what works over time enables them increasingly to 'ask the right questions'. The answers thus generated then inform leaders' decisions about priorities, and as we found earlier in the book, this is half the battle. Priorities are the keys to the gates on the bridge between uncertainty and high performance. Having and displaying the nerve to hold one's balance and find the right keys – even when the bridge is swaying in the winds of change – requires extraordinary leadership. Getting it right consistently soon engenders confidence, not just in the leadership, but in the vision and values that they have held out for the organization. These should endure through all the turbulence of change if they were fundamentally right and well conceived in the first place.

Figure 8.2 shows that whether you are looking at the Excellence Model or a scorecard of the type that gave birth to it, the results criteria or boxes can be mapped fairly easily. Whichever you are using, you will soon find that improvements will depend on *how* things are done. Improving the implementation strategies will get results. Shouting at hamsters to get them to run faster in their wheels rarely does!

Finally, depending on how one uses the scorecard, there may be some 'grey areas' around the edges. For example, the 'internal process' box might include customer-facing processes (such as those performed by a cashier in a bank and assessed by such tools as 'mystery shopping'). These are, in fact, 'lead indicators' of customer satisfaction and so could

Figure 8.2 *The alignment between the balanced scorecard and the EFQM Excellence Model*

arguably be in that box. The message is that understanding the issues is far more important than precise placing. The models are tools for you to use as you wish, not a straitjacket to hog-tie you and get you worried about definitions!

9

Holding the ring – containing anxiety and distress

A leader takes people where they want to go. A great leader takes people where they don't necessarily want to go, but ought to be.

Rosalynn Carter

ANXIETY IS GUARANTEED

Anxiety goes with the territory. People's territory! If organizational changes are imposed – as may seem to be the case from the perspective of many employees, even when the vision for the future is carefully articulated by the leadership – levels of anxiety and even distress are guaranteed to rise. The reaction of most people to any imposed change is to attempt to deny the need for it. They will be able to give lots of reasons why 'it won't work'. They may feel attached to what they currently do and the way they currently do it. They cannot see the reason for change. This situation is bad enough in most honourable and essentially ethical companies and organizations. We are lucky in most of the so-called 'developed world' that such organizations are the norm. Where there are strong vested interests, and where abuse of power and position lead to lucrative opportunities for graft and corruption, it is easy to see how attempting major change can be at best frustrating (when proposed changes are actively thwarted at every step), and at worst downright dangerous for the would-be architects of reform. Unfortunately the scourge of corruption is endemic in many developing countries. This also 'goes with the territory' in the public sector, and in the private sector it would be inconceivable for a salesman in some countries to imagine that he could ever win an order without resorting to the offer of some sort of 'kick-back' to the person with the power and position to place the order.

As plans for the changes emerge people may get understandably depressed and frustrated, trying to defend their 'territory' or their jobs, or they may get even more frustrated at what they feel will be one more useless initiative to move a big boulder with a very small stick. E-commerce has its own share of new versions of such 'turf wars'. Modahl (2000) has some useful pointers for businesses caught up in 'channel conflict' where, for example, existing distributors feel aggrieved and threatened by new direct sales growth via the Internet.

DEALING WITH DIS-EQUILIBRIUM

When considering the characteristic responses of many employees or partners to dis-equilibrium, it is often helpful to look at any experience that the business or organization may have of dealing with such stressful times in the past. In addition to providing historical cultural pointers, this analysis can highlight what mechanisms to regulate stress (or distress) may currently be within the control of leaders. Just as individuals will exhibit predictable 'back-up' behaviours under stress that are the documented counter-points to the normal behaviour of their typical personality type, so organizations can develop a group stress syndrome that is a corollary of their normal prevailing culture, and thus, to some extent, predictable. In many new or non-unionized organizations that have not had to deal with old-style industrial disputes of the type common in the 1970s, there is no corporate memory of the way to a win–win situation in such situations. Even where such experience does exist, completely new and creative thinking will almost certainly be necessary, and this may have to involve deals with existing market channels, or assistance for them to come up to speed with complementary technology systems.

So what are the main barriers or mental blocks that such dysfunctional behaviour exemplifies? They are, of course, well researched and have been well documented by Guirdham (1995), Carnall (1995) and others. Their insights and recommendations for the maintenance of the self-esteem of everyone involved are extremely useful for business leaders – not just MBA students, human resources managers and trainers who tend, unfortunately, to be the main audience for such works.

Zalesnik (1989) goes so far as to suggest that management's fetish for control of the status quo is actually a 'worldview' that is embedded in the corporate group-think of professional managers. The world is a machine to be controlled and the control systems, particularly in hier-archical organizations, enable managers to control people's behaviour. When this control ceases to be in people's best interests it also ceases to be in the best interests of the organization. Zalesnik highlights the need for satisfaction, belonging and identity.

These are basic needs identified long ago by Maslow and captured more recently as we have seen in the balanced scorecard. If these are not provided for and encouraged, and if management appears only to be concerned about the bottom line and the share price, seeing people merely as a resource in this equation, the 'worldview' should eventually be seen to be bankrupt. For this to happen, however, effective leaders will need to step in and coach such managers to a new paradigm and the development of an ethos where the few at the top of the hierarchy really are seen to have the best interests of the majority in mind. Many would say that if this were to happen in their organizations it would indeed be extraordinary! Most organizations have a long way to go.

Whose dis-ease are we talking about?

A newspaper columnist recently commented on a company that was laying off around 2,000 workers to counter the fact that their quarterly results were not going to be up to stock market expectations. The commentator was dreaming of the day when a CEO would stand up and say no to the analysts, and tell them that the business had no intention of laying off people just to satisfy the market's lust for a 20 per cent per annum growth (or ROI or whatever), when by retaining them the firm would be protecting its longer-term future and still delivering 10 per cent. The journalist realized that this was a vain hope in the extreme!

SYMBOLS

Symbols of corporate identity can be extremely powerful cultural rallying points. Nothing is as obvious and as cliché-prone as a flag in this respect and attempting to do away with such symbols just because, for example, two businesses are merging and seeking a new corporate identity, can cause untold adverse reaction. The State of Mississippi recently found that a majority of its citizens wanted passionately to retain a state flag that was highly offensive to many whites and nearly all black African Americans because of its historical associations with the rebel Confederate cause and the discrimination and abuse of human rights that it represented. Despite being seen as an anachronism and a last vestige of 'Dixieland', that any right thinking person from elsewhere might think was easily disposable, the flag obviously represents far more than just nostalgia and homage to heritage.

POWER AND INFLUENCE

Introducing major change must involve the legitimate exercise of power. Details and refinements of strategy may emerge, but the essential progress and direction must be proactively coordinated. The broader a leader's power base is, the more they will be able to influence others in this endeavour. This will be the case provided that the nature of the 'contract' that people believe they hold with the organization is kept constantly under review and seen to be appropriate in terms of current reality. As is often the case, this is about managing expectations. As long as the balance of expectations in this psychological contract is not upset, people will accept a leader's influence. Stacey (1996) points to the need for equilibrium in such situations (as in so many others). He summarizes this succinctly as follows: 'It is in the border area between the equilibrium states of authority, force, power vacuum and impotence that we find power in its form of influence and that is what change requires.'

I suggest that the nature and exercise of influence through extra-ordinary leadership can facilitate the all-important learning that is necessary. Leaders have a responsibility here to create a good enough holding environment for this to happen. This is something of a conundrum or paradox where people must learn to hold the anxiety generated by the very need for rapid and probably continuous learning.

In the event that equilibrium is lost, and confidence along with it, the responsibility for restoring both will fall squarely on the leadership. This is a competence which leaders themselves will often have to learn. We all learn best from experience but we are unable to experience the consequences of many important organizational decisions in advance. Learning laboratories can help to remove this constraint through system dynamics simulation games that compress time and space. Such research may have significant impact on the process of speeding up risk analysis and decision making in many situations. It may prove to have value in the fast-moving world of e-commerce, but in the end a good and instinctive sense of direction and the courage to trust it will probably serve as well as expensive simulations that can only ever work on data you provide anyway. Supplementing instinct with the navigational aids I have proposed in the Toolkit will, I believe, provide as good a 'fix' on the future as any.

Holding the ring

What I believe is more generally necessary is that leaders should give the impression of being well able to hold the dynamic tension between the relatively comforting certainties that are provided by good perform-ance management and total quality management on the one hand, and the unsettling uncertainty of major change and new or emergent strategies on the other. The view from the tower that we described in Chapter 4 should enable leaders to imagine throwing a ring around the totality of this operational dynamic and then, as it were, 'holding the ring'. As I pointed out in Chapter 1, people will generally be pre-pared to take on responsibility for adaptive work towards the ordinary management of better performance, if they can see, or at least feel, that someone is looking after the more extraordinary leadership of the process of managing uncertainty.

THE IMPORTANCE OF THE LEARNING – OR COACHING – ORGANIZATION

Learning organizations represent a significant evolution of organ-izational culture and as such their emergence requires a new set of leadership capabilities. Much of the theory – the knowledge that should prove valuable for underpinning competence development – has been well received, as the success of Peter Senge's works has demonstrated. What is still needed is a 'road map' and 'toolkit' that will enable leaders who wish to facilitate the process in their organizations to do so with the confidence that they would wish to inspire and engender in others. I believe that drawing up this map is probably a communal responsibility. Everyone should regard themselves as potentially able to teach or coach others about things that they have found to be valuable – the 'nuggets' that they have retained when sifting through however few or many years of experience they may have.

As I mentioned in the Introduction, Noel Tichy points out with his reference to the way Special Forces operatives routinely teach newly learnt adaptive or generative skills to their colleagues, regardless of rank or status, that this is a fast way for the team as a whole to learn. It may even ensure their survival. My own experience with Special Forces first taught me that not everyone can or should be a specialist in everything. Small operational teams usually consist of highly trained specialists with a range of many different skills between them. Officers have to endeavour to be 'up to speed' in many disciplines (as do leaders in any environment) but when your life is at stake positional authority should take second place to that of expertise. Young or recently joined Special Forces officers frequently defer to those of lesser rank with no consideration of status-consciousness where specialist skills or knowledge are required in critical situations. It does not in any way diminish their real or perceived authority. In fact lack of preparedness to do this would rapidly erode the trust of their colleagues and ensure that they did not last long in the job.

Situational learning from situational leadership

In the 1940s it was first suggested that leadership is, or should be specific to particular situations and that the selection and characteristics of leaders should be functions of the situation. More recently Ken Blanchard, author of the hugely successful 'One Minute Manager' series of books introduced what he called 'situational leadership', which was actually a development of an original idea that teams or groups facing new challenges will always go through four predictable stages: forming, storming, norming and performing. Blanchard offered an appealing additional sophistication to the original theory by suggesting that leaders should adjust their leadership style to cater for the group's state of mind (and productivity) during each of these stages of team development.

Stages of team development

Initially when facing a new challenge – perhaps when a new project team is formed – the group, while perhaps typically having some degree of apprehension, will be essentially keen, enthusiastic, optimistic, and ready to accept a high degree of direction from their leader. At this stage the productivity will be seen to be initially encouraging as the new team throws itself enthusiastically into new work from a 'green fields' situation. It is still, however, a long way from being a high performance team.

As the group struggles to find appropriate ways of working and as it wrestles with new and unfamiliar challenges and relationships, stresses develop, disillusionment is common, productivity typically drops off, and the group requires a lot of encouragement through coaching from the leadership.

Eventually the group will start to function more as a team. They will begin to learn and respect one another's strengths, and tolerate and support weaknesses in their team mates. They will start to work out the best way to organize processes efficiently and, in thus becoming more self-sufficient, they will require mostly support from the leader and less direction. Productivity will typically rise steadily as team and individual performance improves.

Finally, the work group will weld itself together into a 'high performance team' that, for most purposes, will appear to be self-managing, and to which the leader can safely delegate a high degree of autonomy. But what happens if there is a serious problem?

Blanchard's solution is simple and elegant. He suggests that the leader must adjust his or her own style and make it appropriate to the regression of the team's state of mind, its confidence, and its failing performance or productivity under stress. He predicts that teams in difficulties will regress through the same stages of development, and that accordingly delegation must give way to more support, more coaching, and if necessary even more direction. In other words, the leader must be sensitive to the situation, flexible and able to diagnose at any time where the whole team (or perhaps individual members) are on their development continuum, adjusting his or her own leadership style accordingly. This theory is neat; it reflects many people's experience, and it lends itself wonderfully as a model for use by trainers in team-building programmes. It is, in fact, a nice development of Adair's simpler model, and it pre-empted the 'learning organization' concept of the whole organization having to learn to be similarly flexible in its dealings with an increasingly complex operating environment where business (and life) was one big change project. The overall learning quotient of the organization is enhanced through the leader's effectiveness as teacher and coach.

I would have one caveat, however. I do not think that Blanchard would ever have meant to suggest that the role of the leader in all of this should be as reactive as my brief description of his theory might imply. Directing, coaching, supporting and empowering the whole organization must be primarily a proactive role and not a matter of reacting either to new situations or to employees' discomfort, although leaders must do both of these things when necessary. I believe that we are probably talking more about required new leadership competencies than about leadership styles. To cope with the complexity of leading others in what may typically be a whole range of change 'projects' at various stages of development is extraordinarily difficult and it is the work, and the responsibility, of extraordinary leadership.

Getting it right will produce definite quantifiable benefits. Let us consider what the 'outputs' of the process of developing a 'learning organization culture' could be. They need to be seen as potentially beneficial by all of the 'stakeholders', whose engagement and 'ownership' will be needed if progress towards their achievement is to be project managed and ideally benchmarked.

Potential benefits of learning – 'the 10 Cs' of the coaching organization

1. *Confidence* – in the knowledge that appropriate leadership style can role model a soundly based, balanced and holistic approach to organizational performance improvement.

2. *Clarity and consistency of purpose and direction* – developing a shared vision for strategic change (including new e-business development), and the means to convert it into effective action. Belief in the compass, if not the map.

3. *Communication tools* – to help leaders communicate the message and potential benefits of the change vision in every way possible throughout the organization and to all stakeholders.

4. *Creation of 'quick wins'* – managers will know how to plan for them (rather than just hope they will happen), and how to recognize and reward those people at all levels who help to bring them about.

5. *Caring* – enhanced employee satisfaction through human resource development policies, and strategies for the achievement of results through commitment and empowerment.

6. *Customer focus* – recognition of the essential importance of this element for effective service delivery, and how to make it central to the strategic and operational planning process. Recognition of the completely new phenomenon of companies' Internet marketing strategies driving customer behaviour rather than the other way round. Basing these strategies partly on the new data mining/warehousing technologies and technographics research, and remembering that a customer is an equally valuable customer, whether traditionally or technologically acquired!

7. *Cause and effect linkages* – added value from learning how to monitor and evaluate improvement initiatives, benchmark measurable improvements, identify trends, and learn from the results; particularly those relating to customers.

8. *Continuous learning from continuous improvement* – discovering that continuous improvement produces continuous learning produces continuous improvement – and so on in a virtuous cycle.

9. *Corporate citizenship* – the benefits of enhancing society's perception of the organization and the unprecedented opportunities for doing so that are provided by the Internet for both private and public sector organizations.

10. *Credibility* – consolidating the gains and sustaining the momentum.

The vital step in the establishment and building of this process is that of handing responsibility for these outputs of adaptive and increasingly generative work back to those whose confidence should, through good leadership, be enhanced sufficiently to thrive on the challenge. The benefits will be apparent when people are increasingly seen to do this, rather than simply to cope with change, or worse, feel threatened by it. This progressive and desirable paradigm shift is the subject of the next chapter.

10

The cultural perspective

Good leaders make people feel that they're at the very heart of things, not at the periphery. Everyone feels that he or she makes a difference to the success of the organization. When that happens people feel centred and that gives their work meaning.

Warren Bennis

NECESSARY PROGRESSION

The previous chapters have explained how leaders need to create a learning environment where their people can be developed to take more responsibility for the work that is necessary to make changes happen. Typically managers and employees have to progress (in a way not dissimilar from that described by Blanchard in his situational leadership model) from dependency to engagement to commitment to quality ownership. They do this through a shared vision, coaching, empowerment and learning.

The concept of this progression, this 'process' we would like leaders to lead, and their responsibility for doing so, is widely accepted. Peter Senge quotes a well-known Chief Executive Officer (Hanover Insurance's William O'Brien) as saying:

If this type of organization is so widely preferred, why don't people create such organizations? I think the answer is leadership. People have no real comprehension of the type of commitment it requires to build such an organization.

Senge goes on to suggest that in learning organizations leaders' roles differ dramatically from that of the charismatic decision maker who could not create such an organization all on his or her own anyway. He suggests that the new role requires skills of designing, teaching and stewarding so that a vision of a better future state can provide the incentive that will pull people and the organization through uncertainty and perhaps adversity. This view is endorsed by Haines (1995), who describes an effective leadership triangle where the key roles should now be those of trainer, coach and facilitator. Both of these leadership style models are shown as essentially opposed to the problem-solving orientation of putting things right to get away from an analysis of unfortunate current reality (while still having to worry about the uncertainty of the future). Senge does not suggest, however, that stewardship of a vision, or encouraging others to make executive decisions based on it, will be sufficient without a lot of hard work or 'commitment', as his source O'Brien puts it.

Grand knowing and salesmanship?

To amplify this point, Heifetz and Laurie (1997) are of the opinion that:

the prevailing notion that leadership consists of having a vision and aligning people with that vision is bankrupt because it continues to treat adaptive situations as if they were technical: the authority figure is supposed to divine where the company is going and people are supposed to follow. Leadership is reduced to a combination of grand knowing and salesmanship.

They go on to say that leadership has, in fact, to take place every day and that, 'one can lead with no more than a question in hand'.

At this point, I will play the Devil's Advocate. One suspects that many seasoned practitioners will be tempted to say: 'This is all very well; but if Professor Senge and Professor Heifetz were to put themselves in the place of the CEO of an ailing auto-manufacturer, or the head of the civil service in a bankrupt "developing" country, what would we see them actually doing to put these undoubtedly visionary ideas into useful practice?' There probably is no sense of urgency, let alone a vision, and if there is something like a vision, it probably wasn't arrived at by proper consensus, and it probably isn't communicated adequately. How would they role model the 'designer-teacher-steward' or 'trainer-coach-facilitator' competencies? How would they 'lead with no more than a question in hand'?

The first thing they would have to do would be to gain some understanding of the prevailing culture – the paradigm – 'the way people do things (and probably always have) around here'. This would undoubtedly prove to be the single most important aspect of the current reality, away from which the organization was waiting (no doubt less than eagerly) to be led. It would also be the source of the greatest inertia against creative progress, and the greatest resistance, in the forms of all the barriers that people are capable of erecting in the way of that progress when they see it as threatening to their perceived interests.

Having 'no more than a question in hand' might leave one somewhat exposed if others failed to see just how visionary the question was, or worse, if they perceived it as mischievous or threatening to their interests or their 'territory'. So despite denying that executive decision making (in pursuit of a vision) still has a role to play in the new scheme of things, one might well find that someone (or perhaps some group or 'guiding coalition' as John Kotter puts it), must decide effectively to 'propose' and/or get agreement for the organizational vision and then 'drive' the process of working towards it. The lack of a sense of urgency to do what a few visionary people can see to be necessary is usually an important element of the current reality. Furthermore, it will be a predictable cause of failure of any change programmes, (as Kotter points out), if someone (ie a leader or the corporate leadership team) fails to take executive decisions to programme the process of change. I cannot see why there should be anything politically or fashionably incorrect about this point of view.

Actions based on such decisions initially have to be to raise the sense of urgency, and then determinedly to 'sell' the vision of a better future state of affairs. The vision may well be one that is originally articulated by some particularly bright or visionary individual who is not necessarily the 'leader'. Nor may such an individual be in a position to wield authority or influence without the sponsorship of someone who is both powerful enough and imaginative enough to see the importance and urgency of the problem and sponsor its potential solution. The existence of a suitably creative and empowering environment to facilitate such linkages is, of course, the key catalyst for change here, and its creation and development is itself an important part of the extraordinary leader's remit.

DECISIONS, DECISIONS

In Chapter 6 I quoted Alistair Mant's description of the decision-making process which he describes as 'the anatomy of timely decision making'. He implies that more often than not leaders must rely on their instincts for what are the right things to do in any given circumstance.

The problem-solving competence is here used, not so much to generate the energy to get away from an aspect of current reality that is undesirable, as to energize the process of planning, prioritizing and implementing across-the-board performance improvements or perhaps necessary new and bold ventures into e-business. In either case they will need to be integrated to involve and engage all the 'excellence enablers' we mentioned in Chapter 8. These in turn will produce incremental and measurable progress towards the envisioned future state, and this will engender confidence in both the leadership and the vision they have held out for the organization. Indeed, even the chosen approaches, the deployment of leadership behaviours, and leaders' decision making in respect of the definition of which processes will be critical in this pursuit of improved results, can themselves be the subject of review and self-assessment along the way by the executive management team.

The way to change or shift paradigms is by project managing this self-assessment and other parts of a planned performance management systems improvement programme. This is the way for leaders to address the management of performance and the management of uncertainty at the same time. By engaging everyone in the integrated elements of the process, they will be role modelling systems thinking and holding the 'creative tension' that Peter Senge describes elsewhere in his writing as being necessary.

SHIFTING PARADIGMS

We hear a lot about paradigm shift, and I have used the words myself as if we all share a common understanding of just what we mean by them. Stephen Covey (1992) suggests that when Peters and Waterman's book *In Search of Excellence* (1988) took the United States and the rest of the management world by storm, it was because the time had come for the idea and the ideals contained in it. He goes on to suggest that:

> *it's now high time for many individuals and companies to make a quantum leap in performance, a healthy change of habits, a major shift in patterns; otherwise it's business as usual and that's simply not cutting it anymore.*

If a culture of generating and sustaining high performance is indeed the 'what?' that describes the new paradigm, what then is the 'how'? How do you become more effective? According to Covey the solution is nothing short of revolutionary and requires a complete change of people's frame of reference, or 'worldview'. He suggests that all great breakthroughs are, and have been, breaks with old ways of thinking:

> *I have found that if you want to make slow incremental improvement, change your attitude or behavior. But if you want to improve in major ways – I mean dramatic, revolutionary, transforming ways – if you want to make quantum improvements, either as an individual or as an organization, change your frame of reference. Change how you see the world, how you think about people, how you view your management and leadership. Change your 'paradigm', your scheme for understanding and explaining certain aspects of reality.*

It is interesting to consider to what extent it may be possible, or indeed a required competence, for leaders to divine when the time is right for new ideas, if Covey is correct. This would need to be just ahead of time, as it were, and form part of a vision that they can communicate as Peters and Waterman apparently did with *In Search of Excellence*. Having this foresight can inspire leaders with the sense of urgency that they will clearly then need to communicate to others. Tom Peters' writings are imbued with an all-pervading sense of urgency that he succeeds in making compelling. There will always be many cases, however, where even the most visionary of insights prove incomplete, or simply flawed, and when unforeseen problems are consequently thrust upon you. In such cases the approach probably has to be more a combination of instinctive and analytical decision making, with a feedback loop that builds organizational learning about the new challenge.

What I believe to be essential in this understanding of the way to view a current paradigm, is that one must never fall into the trap of thinking that the 'single best way' is somehow out there, and that what are now seen as best practices and innovative techniques will necessarily provide the keys to uncertainty. I have carefully chosen models and techniques in this book that I believe are capable of standing the test of time – at least for the time being. They will help leaders to identify what may be revolutionary new ways (given the current paradigm) of improving performance in their organizations. As such they will help leaders to identify priorities based on a true sense of direction. The priorities are, in fact, the keys, and as each one succeeds in unlocking another aspect of an uncertain future, it will subtly help to shift the paradigm.

Despite the use of words such as 'revolutionary', and however great the sense of urgency, it will normally be unwise – and a technique of last resort – to attempt to 'smash' the existing paradigm. Even (and perhaps especially) in cases where it is clearly bankrupt, outdated, reactionary and counterproductive, many people will be attached to it and will have established personal paradigms that benefit from the status quo. One is reminded once again of Newton's Third Law: every action has an equal and opposite reaction.

THE POWER OF PURPOSE AND PRINCIPLES

People will not be impressed by new tricks, tools and methodologies being imposed upon them like some form of medication. If such initiatives are seen to be led by consultants from outside the organization, the resistance will probably be even greater and all sorts of suspicions and rumours will flourish concerning the real reasons for the 'change' programme, the re-engineering, or the endless training courses. If the existing paradigm really is outdated and an impediment to performance improvement, ways must be found to empower people first to improve their own satisfaction with their work. Once again Covey puts it succinctly:

> _People want to contribute to the accomplishment of worthwhile objectives._
> _They want to be part of a mission and enterprise that transcends their_
> _individual tasks. They don't want to work in a job that has little meaning,_
> _even though it may tap their mental capacities. They want purposes and_
> _principles that lift them, ennoble them, inspire them, empower them,_
> _and encourage them to their best-selves._

Where they don't find these stimuli and these opportunities it is a failure of the leadership. Where they not only settle for the existing outdated paradigm, but dig into it for protection, it is because nobody has painted a picture of the future for them that is more compelling than the one they hold of the present. Where leaders do succeed in motivating others to raise their own performance to fulfil their potential, extraordinary business results, extraordinary customer satisfaction, extraordinary employee satisfaction, and an extraordinarily positive impact on society usually follow.

While I have said elsewhere that the mechanics of operating a performance management system can be considered to be 'ordinary management', there is no doubt that any such system – even one evidencing all the features of internationally recognized best practice – will only be as good as the leadership's determination to take it seriously and ensure that others throughout the organization do likewise. People should understand from the start that the system as a whole is primarily developmental both for the organization and for individuals. Sustaining high performance requires an integrated system of initiatives and methodologies, but most of all it requires dedicated leadership by senior executives prepared to role model the values, principles and competencies that the desired culture and operating paradigm enshrine.

The culture of an organization is in effect a composite and unwritten social contract. As such it is more powerful than any written performance contracts or even an unwritten but individual psychological one. The performance management system must be sympathetic to this and integrated with all other components of the wider organizational system, taking into account both its internal corporate and external market or customer perspectives. The next chapter describes such a system.

Part IV

Leading extraordinary perfomance

11

Planning for extraordinary performance

We could not in a lifetime exhaust the possibilities provided by the innovative use of people and information.

Sun Tzu

LEADERSHIP RESPONSIBILITY FOR PERFORMANCE

I have included this guide to the planning process because I believe that the influence and practical application of good leadership is essential if strategic and operational or business planning are to be worthwhile and effective. Equally, no system for performance appraisal, even one that attempts to be developmental and non-threatening, will be of any use unless leaders at all levels take it seriously and are prepared to use it to support a paradigm of empowerment and accountability. This chapter is not a comprehensive set of highly technical instructions for the strategic planning process, and the next chapter is not either although it offers advice on the establishment of an appraisal system. Plenty of other textbooks provide this. Rather it is a synopsis of what I have found to be useful for leaders to understand about a process that I believe requires their personal and visible involvement and engagement. Leaders simply cannot delegate responsibility for this process to a planning unit or some editorial group. The head of the civil service in one country where I worked actually abolished just such a planning secretariat after he had asked the principal permanent secretary (the equivalent of the CEO) of a certain ministry how he was getting on with his new five-year medium-term strategic plan. The reply was, 'I don't know; you'd better ask the secretariat.'

PERFORMANCE MANAGEMENT – A SYSTEMS APPROACH

It is important to know what performance management is, but we also need to know what it is not. For it to be successfully introduced and implemented in any organization, managers and employees at all levels need to be aware of some common misconceptions that can trip up the unwary, or become the source of unnecessary concerns and resistance. I am grateful to Canadian performance management expert and author Robert Bacal and his publishers for ideas from his excellent guide on the subject (Bacal, 1999).

Performance management is not:

▌ something a manager does to an employee;

▌ a big stick to force people to work better or harder;

▌ cost–benefit analysis;

▌ used only in poor performance situations;

▌ about completing forms once a year.

What it is, on the other hand, is simply an integrated set of mechanisms and processes that facilitate better communication and understanding between people who work together. It's about people working with others to add value to each other's contributions in the pursuit of continuous improvement in results and standards. If this can be achieved for the organization as a whole it will almost certainly make everyone's individual situation better as well. Everyone wins if employees are directed and supported so that they can work as effectively and efficiently as possible *in line with the needs of their customers, and the needs of the organization that should serve these customers.* This involves establishing clear expectations and understanding about results to be achieved and the jobs to be done to achieve them. It is a system. That is, it has a number of parts, all of which need to be included, refined, managed and above all *led*, if it is going to add value to the organization, managers and staff.

The Performance Management System (PMS) mix

We can build an effective performance management system (PMS) through the combination of a variety of tools and interventions at different levels in the organization. These may include, for example:

▌ strategic planning;

▌ the definition of organizational goals, priorities and values, usually summarized in vision and mission statements;

▌ SMART objectives (specific, measurable, achievable and agreed, results-oriented and relevant, time-bound);

▌ the identification, agreement and application of appropriate performance indicators and measures for the organization, for key processes, for functions, and for individual employees;

▌ management team (or departmental) self-assessment processes against benchmarks of recognized good practice and for monitoring and evaluation of continuous improvement;

▌ individual performance review and appraisal;

▌ personal development planning;

▌ learning and development activities;

▌ various forms of incentives that can link performance to budgets (and possibly greater control over them) for divisions, departments, or business units, and to remuneration for the individuals who help to bring about improvements in productivity, service delivery or efficiency.

In the private sector, the precise mix of these different activities may vary from one commercial company to another depending on their perceived corporate needs and objectives. There is clear merit, however, in some form of prescriptive guidelines to inform policy in any public service authority if senior public servants are to manage coordinated and measurable improvements in service delivery. This is particularly so where promises are made to the public through Client Service or Citizens' Charters, and where the standards of service delivery are to be benchmarked and reported.

Neither running public services nor running a company is a programme or a project. It is a profession or vocation. Improving these organizations and the quality of their service delivery, however, will require programme management to manage the process. The process suggested by Professor John Kotter, which I have outlined in Chapter 5, is an admirable model in this context and pays due attention to the essential need to address potential sustainability in everything you need to try to do. It also underlines the need for committed and exemplary leadership of the process if it is to achieve its objectives. This leadership dimension is distinct from, but certainly not divorced from the specific job of project managing interventions at each stage of the process.

THE BENEFITS

What is the potential payoff for using performance management? While performance management cannot solve every problem, it has the potential to address many common management concerns. Robert Bacal suggests that if you use it properly, invest the time, and create cooperative relationships, performance management can:

▪ reduce your need to be involved in everything that goes on (micromanagement);

▪ save time by helping employees make decisions on their own; ensuring they have the necessary knowledge and understanding to make these decisions properly;

▪ reduce time-consuming misunderstandings among staff about who is responsible for what;

▪ reduce the frequency of situations where you don't have the information you need when you need it;

■ reduce mistakes and errors (and their repetition) by helping you and your staff identify the causes of errors or inefficiencies;

■ help staff to identify, understand and agree any gaps that may exist between desirable and actual standards of performance;

■ provide a framework to change a command and blame culture into one that encourages dialogue about organizational and individual development needs and solutions.

Bacal summarizes it all by saying:

Performance management is an investment 'up front' so that you can encourage and allow staff to do their jobs. They will know what they are expected to do, what decisions they can make on their own, how well they have to do their jobs, and when you need to be involved. This will allow you to attend to the tasks that only you can address.

It will certainly not happen overnight but eventually this investment in people can help leaders to delegate more and more authority for the management of performance, which most people will actually welcome. In this way, leaders can spend more time thinking about how they can manage the uncertainty and turbulence of a rapidly changing operating environment, which is something with which most people are not so comfortable. This can save time and money. It can reduce anxiety and distress as we have seen, and it can encourage empowerment of people at all levels to take on the adaptive work that is needed to bring about major change, shifts in outdated paradigms and corporate or organizational development. Modelling the behaviour necessary to do this is called leadership. It is one more example of the type of leadership that is now required in 21st-century organizations, and that I have called 'extraordinary leadership'.

WRITING THE STRATEGIC PLAN

I have indicated that strategic planning – or a strategic plan – is really the first plank or component of an integrated performance management system. When doing the analytical work, and attempting to synthesize ideas that are generated for the plan, it will usually be helpful if the senior management team (perhaps with the assistance of some key stakeholders) can use one or both of the methodological tools that I introduced in Chapters 6 and 7: the Mindworks Approach and the Excellence Model respectively. Both of these will help to provide a systemic overview of all of the key results areas that are required, together with the enabling processes and interventions that should ensure their achievement.

When they are finally ready to attempt to draft the final document, the executive team should first agree a Table of Contents for the strategic plan before a draft is prepared. To a large extent the Table of Contents will reflect the steps of the strategic planning process – or rather, the outputs of these. There are likely to be some minor variations from department to department if such business or organizational sub-units are large enough to need their own strategic plans, but it is obviously advantageous for all to adopt a common terminology to minimize confusion or misinterpretation, especially concerning the hierarchy of objectives and means of measuring achievement. This glossary of terms can and probably should be 'set' by the corporate leadership at the head office of the organization, otherwise there will always be confusion about exactly what is meant by an objective, a target, and so on.

I have included a suggested standard Table of Contents below. The eight proposed chapters or sections incorporate an augmented 'hierarchy of objectives' and contain all the elements required for an organization's strategic plan:

1. Introduction

2. Situation analysis including 'bridges and barriers'

3. Vision and mission

4. Key results areas (KRAs) and their associated goals

5. Strategic objectives (SOs)

6. Strategies

7. Key factors indicating the need for organizational development, change, or reform

8. Action planning to include the outputs and service delivery targets (SDTs) for the three- or five-year medium-term plan period which act as a link to developing annual operational plans and budgets.

The situation analysis

The analytical work and the synthesis of ideas for this will have been done in workshops, possibly using the Mindworks Approach and/or the Excellence Model. The real adaptive work of implementation should, of course, follow and be scheduled into the successive operating plans. A summary should be presented, perhaps in the form of the well-known and understood SWOT analysis showing strengths, weaknesses, opportunities and threats. This tool could, of course, be used in the actual analytical work as well, but the two models I have suggested will provide a more comprehensive and rigorous analysis, particularly of the 'softer' areas such as customer and employee satisfaction.

Key results areas (KRAs) and goals

The KRAs are the 'main whats' from the Mindworks analysis. As these key results areas are necessarily worded generally, it is usually advisable to have at least one goal for each KRA but there could be more. For example, if a KRA refers to sales or market penetration that must be achieved both in home and export markets, there could possibly be two goals attached to it. The goals describe the main area of activity or service and may indicate the quality or standard to which the organization aspires to deliver them in the medium term, for example: 'The provision of clear, concise and timely information, data and guidelines to clients and stakeholders on technology investment strategy matters.'

Strategic objectives (SOs)

Strategic objectives must be essentially 'strategic'. That is to say, they should not contain references to the minutiae of the activities necessary to achieve their often multiple component 'outputs'. It is necessary to ensure that they are worded in such a way as to clarify or ensure that they are achievable within the three- or five-year time frame of the plan. However, it is not necessary to be too concerned to make them fully SMART in the same way as it definitely _is_ necessary to do for their component elements, which we will call 'outputs'. In effect the KRAs will be time-bound within the parameters of the medium-term plan, whether it be for three or perhaps five years. They will, one hopes, be agreed by the executive team, and they will be specific enough to warrant their own separate identity and associated 'goals'.

Outputs

Outputs (the specific component elements of strategic objectives) *must* be measurable, and they *must* be time-bound. In fact, as well as being featured in the strategic plan, they will be scheduled within the particular operational planning year (of the medium-term plan period) during which they are expected to be achieved. As such they will also be linked to budget, ie the inputs which are necessary for the activities required for their achievement will be costed, and the necessary expenditure scheduled with proper line management accountability.

Accountability

The accountability for *outputs* derived from the strategic objectives should be designated in whatever equates to departmental terms in the strategic plan. This is as far as this medium-term plan should go where operational detail is concerned. It does no harm, however, to name individuals at this level in an attached matrix annex. This is because responsibility and accountability for the achievement of certain SOs and their respective outputs should be placed at the door of those senior managers whose departments, divisions or perhaps business units will be required to deliver them. They should also be reflected in the form of personal objectives for these managers in performance agreements or perhaps even performance contracts.

The link to annual operating or annual business plans

The hierarchy of objectives for the annual operating plans or business plans that derive from the strategic plan will effectively start with outputs, perhaps grouping them under their respective strategic objectives. The outputs will, in turn, break down further into activities and inputs. It is at this stage that the link to budget is established because the estimated costs of these inputs need to be included.

Performance indicators (PIs) and service delivery targets (SDTs)

We mentioned that outputs must be SMART. It is at this point in the document where the agreement (A) about the way in which they will, in fact, be specific (S), measurable (M), realistic (R) and timed (T) should be captured. For example, it is no good having an output that simply says you are going to train people. You (and all those affected by the plan and its costs) need to know how many people, to what standard, and by what date. If someone said they wanted to be a millionaire you would probably laugh and not take much notice. If they said that they needed £975,000 by 3 o'clock tomorrow afternoon, you would probably take an interest because it sounds serious!

Drafting the document

The drafting can, and probably should, be delegated to a planning unit if the business is large enough to have one, but it should be seen as important enough for senior managers to have close scrutiny, and probably leadership of this team. In any event, the result should be seen as a line management responsibility. If two or three team members share the writing, possibly by taking specific chapters, it will reduce the workload and the time taken to prepare the draft. Doing so should be relatively straightforward because all of the strategic thinking will have already been done during workshops using the Mindworks Approach and/or the Excellence Model balanced scorecard. The raw material for the strategic planning document will be contained in the workshop notes, ideas and flipchart pads that will have been collected throughout this process. The job of those drafting the document is to put in some connecting words, sentences and paragraphs to bind together the substance of the plan that has been created and make it readable and 'user-friendly'.

The final document must be 'user-friendly' if it is to be regarded as a working document and not gather dust on the shelf. At this stage the substance of the plan should not be changed. It will undoubtedly be useful and helpful to produce an annex or appendix in the form of a matrix showing the logical hierarchy of the KRAs, goals and strategic objectives, together with their strategies and service delivery targets including key performance indicators and the responsibilities/account-abilities of divisional or departmental managers. This is a form of logical framework rather like the one that I have proposed and recommended later for the annual operating plan. At the level of the strategic plan it will not, however, need to cascade as far as the actual planned activities and the budgeted cost of their respective inputs.

We have necessarily introduced a certain amount of what could be called jargon here, but the context should make the various words self-explanatory and I stress that establishing a 'once and for all' terminology is necessary to avoid confusion. It is important to make sure that the 'authors' avoid any further jargon that may be specific to the organ-ization or sector. Although the document belongs to the business or organization, the main body of it, which will not be confidential, should probably be reviewed by stakeholders who are technically outsiders, and they need to understand what the plan is trying to communicate. Any elements that are sensitive can be placed in separate appendices with limited circulation. The writers should use plain and simple English. If the corporate policy is to publish the plan document in English where this is not the native language (as it is now the official business language in so many parts of the world), it may be an additional benefit if the text can ultimately be checked and edited by a native English speaker, provided one with the necessary understanding of the subject matter is available.

Before the drafting team takes over, the executive team or strategy group should make sure that a date is agreed when the editors should present the draft. The editors should circulate the draft to members of the strategy group before this group meets again to discuss it. If consultants or facilitators have been used to catalyse the strategic thinking process they need not necessarily be present at this meeting unless the team explicitly asks them to be there. It should be possible to agree any changes to the draft at a single meeting, but if this is not feasible, the team should set itself a deadline to finish the 'comments' stage. Finally the editors should be requested to produce a final version, again by an agreed date.

Sample contents of a strategic plan

1. Introduction A short description of the approach adopted, including references to previous work and plans, or projects that have informed the plan's production.

2. Situation Analysis A synopsis of the current situation of the organization, including reference to critical issues likely to affect the achievement of objectives, and identified 'bridges and barriers'.

3. Vision and Mission How the business sees its role, values and future organizational culture, and a summary statement of what it actually hopes to achieve in the medium-term period covered by the plan.

4. Key Results Areas The strategic areas where customers, clients and other stakeholders require, or have a right to expect, results from the organization.

5. Strategic Objectives What the business wishes specifically to accomplish in the next five years. The specific constituent elements of the KRAs.

6. Strategies How the business expects to achieve its mission and objectives. It is usually helpful to include a brief statement of the broad strategy for delivering each KRA, and also for each SO.

7. Key Factors What factors will help and which will hinder the business in achieving its mission and objectives. These will have been identified in the 'bridges and barriers' step of the Mindworks Approach analysis. A summary of conclusions about what can be done to reduce the barriers and make use of the bridges, together with any perceived priorities for change. (These may form the basis for a KRA which will be additional to those concerned with the organization's mainstream functions and can incorporate objectives for strategic change and reform.)

8. Action Plan This sets out the necessary activities broken down into their constituent SMART outputs, with departmental responsibilities (accountabilities) and dates, for converting the strategy into action. This should include a summary of key performance indicators and departmental service delivery targets which are the link to developing annual operating or business plans and budgets.

CONNECTING THE PLANNING TO THE PEOPLE

In Chapter 7 we began to consider the real challenge: how to translate a vision for a better future state – even one which is effectively 'sold' to the people – into the adaptive work that they themselves must engage in to actualize it. We saw that the holistic design concept of the Excellence Model (or any of the internationally proven balanced scorecard systems) can act as a framework for all improvement initiatives or a checklist to remind managers of vital interdependencies of the various organs of the 'frog'. Earlier we saw how it could be used specifically to frame a picture of the future and an analysis of the current reality. We saw how the product of this analysis could be as many as 150 areas for improvement (AFIs) that must be addressed when we attempt the 'leap into the future'. We also noted that out of these a 'vital few' would need to be selected for inclusion in operating plans (more leadership group decision making here!).

Now it is time to relate the paperwork to the people; time in fact to give the problem back to them so that they can solve it by programming the adaptive (and sometimes generative) work that is needed to effect the necessary improvements and make change happen. Their involvement, engagement, commitment, and subsequently their creativity and problem solving, will subtly shift the paradigm, as we saw in the last chapter. The vision alone is not the desired paradigm. The paradigm is the attitude of mind that will find creative ways to facilitate its actualization.

Once people believe and trust that the vision is not only appropriate and desirable, but also necessary, achievable and within their capabilities, they will themselves realize that aligning principles, roles and goals with processes and procedures is clearly also necessary. They will realize that they have to make their behaviour congruent with belief, and provided that the leadership has role modelled this behaviour pattern throughout, they will happily emulate and then personify it.

What they will then seek and welcome are models or tools to help them apply a disciplined approach to managing the process and work of the changes. We have already seen how the Mindworks Approach concept, outlined in Chapter 6, for facilitating the strategic thinking process with management teams, can be used to take workshop participants through a customer-focused analysis to derive main whats, whys, and hows, which become key results areas, strategic objectives and strategies respectively for a strategic plan. The use of the Excellence

Model (as mentioned earlier and explained fully in Chapter 8) can help with this. It ensures that the 'picture of the future' and that of 'current reality' take into account all of the 'softer' considerations. These may not easily and logically fall out of a simple analysis based on the organization's original mandate, its articles of association, or even its recognized existing functions, its current structure, or its leaders' vision.

New objectives for new work

For example, identified areas for improvement, derived from the criteria of customer satisfaction, employee satisfaction, or impact on society, should be rationalized with more operationally based key performance objectives. In this way managers can ensure that planned outputs and activities to address these 'softer' systemic results areas relate logically to existing strategic objectives, or perhaps indicate a need for new and additional key results areas and strategic objectives for new adaptive work.

New objectives might specifically address the implementation of necessary changes or reforms. In this way, for example, a thorough analysis of all the implications of an e-business venture or transformation may well throw up completely new requirements. In terms of the plan, these might include the need for a strategic key results area specifically for this new venture. There will also be a multitude of more operationally specific and cross-cutting new inputs and outputs in all existing areas of the business or organization that will be affected by the new strategic developments. In any event there will undoubtedly be far more AFIs than can reasonably be factored into a one-year business or operating plan. Some difficult prioritizing will be necessary and this is particularly the case when you are attempting to decide just how much of your impressive medium-term strategic plan you can hope to achieve in each (and specifically the first) year of operations that is to be derived from it.

Quick wins

As John Kotter reminded us in his eight-stage model for leading the change process, it is extremely useful for establishing and sustaining the momentum of this process if some 'quick wins' can be achieved. You will recall, however, that Kotter was at pains to point out that you cannot just hope for these quick wins. You have to create them. The analysis using the Excellence Model will, as we have seen, typically produce between 100 and 150 AFIs (at least 10 to 20 per component of the model).

Balance across the system

The first suggestion, therefore, when looking for the vital few priorities to be included in the one-year operating plan, is to try to include at least one or two from each component area of the model. This will ensure that you continue to pay due attention to the need for systems thinking and balance in your continuous improvement efforts. Even two from each would give you 18 AFIs to work on and for which you would need to ensure suitable outputs, inputs, performance indicators and service delivery targets in your operating plan. The next suggestion is one that can perhaps help you to identify the areas where a 'quick win' might be feasible, and its logic is illustrated in the diagram below. Draw a simple four-box grid (what would consultants do without them?) and attempt to map impact against cost, and then impact against ease of implementation. Any improvement initiatives that are potentially capable of producing results fairly easily and at reasonable cost are potential 'quick wins' and especially important if they are likely to have a significant impact. What is significant in terms of impact is, of course, a matter for the executive team but it could include market penetration, publicity, profitability, or positive effects for the momentum of the change process and for the desired new paradigm.

Box 11.1 *Impact against cost*

High Impact Low Cost	High Impact High Cost
Low Impact Low Cost	Low Impact High Cost

It probably goes without saying that you should forget about any AFIs that are potentially low impact and high cost. Those that are low impact and low cost may be attempted if time and resources permit. Those that are potentially high impact and high cost should certainly not be discarded because they are probably strategically important. Look for 'quick wins' in the high impact/low cost box.

Box 11.2 *Impact against ease of implementation*

High Impact Easy to Implement	High Impact Hard to Implement
Low Impact Easy to Implement	Low Impact Hard to Implement

Once again, it should be easy to decide not to allocate resources to difficult measures that will have low impact, but just because they are hard to do does not mean you should automatically exclude attention to those AFIs that will also have high impact. If time and resources permit you could include some that will have low impact if they are really easy to implement, but you should look for 'quick wins' in the high impact/easy to implement box. Of course there are likely to be very few!

Do not be so focused on the quick wins that you miss the usefulness of this analysis for longer-term strategic advantage. I alluded earlier to the fact that in personal time management it is dangerous to spend all your time on things that appear to be both urgent and important, with the result that you never have enough time for the things that are important but less urgent. Similarly, this analysis can help you to identify those AFIs that are likely to have a big impact but may perhaps be difficult, expensive, or time-consuming to implement. They are probably 'big stones'. Clearly some form of incremental progress should be made with these during the course of the medium-term plan period. Outputs and associated incremental indicators and targets relating to this must be worded in a way that takes care of the progressive nature of this process through the course of successive annual operating plans.

The logical framework

The next new model to be introduced here will be a suggested design for a logical framework matrix, or 'logframe' as it is frequently known. This is a matrix tool for scheduling the performance indicators, service delivery targets, costs and accountabilities of the inputs which will cumulatively form the annual operating plans (or business plans) to be derived from the strategic plan. Such logical frameworks have been used for a number of years as a project management tool. They have been endorsed and adopted by most of the world's major multilateral and bilateral development agencies because, when used effectively, they require the engagement of stakeholders and their active involvement in the planning and agreement of reforms, initiatives or activities that will affect them or their interests.

It is less common to see the use of logical frameworks in normal business planning. It is increasingly the case, however, that many organizations will, either by design or by default, be operating with a matrix management structure. Because they will frequently be orchestrating new ventures or new developments, accommodating acquisitions or planning the launch of new products and services, they will often have several 'projects' on the go at any given time. They will, in effect, almost certainly be running the whole business or organization more like a complex change programme then ever before. Frequently the individual managers and staff involved in these projects or programme components will report to their official line managers and to temporary project managers at the same time. The new e-venture, whether it is an Internet dotcom launch or a transformational augmentation of an existing and established business, is a classic case in point. Here is a 'project', if ever there was one, that needs to be project managed as such, and integrated into mainstream operations in a thoroughly professional way.

Engaging stakeholders in the logframe team

It is always advisable if possible to engage stakeholders (for example some junior managers and possibly partner organizations such as suppliers and distributors) in a team approach to the construction of the logframe that will govern actual implementation of the adaptive work in which we want them to be involved. The membership of the group that is put together for this purpose is really a matter for the senior executive team of the business or organization. It could perhaps include key supplier or distributor partners, and certainly line managers who will be required to 'sign up' to the agreed outputs, indicators and targets.

Figure 11.1 shows a template for a typical logframe. It has a hierarchy of objectives just as the strategic plan does, but one that extends right down to the identification of individual activities and their associated and costed inputs. In this case the vertical logic of this cascade of objectives is complemented with a horizontal logic that captures the objectively verifiable performance indicators for each of these objectives. The methods by which these indicators will be verified or measured, and finally any risks and assumptions that have been considered to be relevant to the likelihood of success and sustainability, are also included on the horizontal axis of the matrix.

Business or organization.........................
Medium-term strategic plan year..............
Operating plan year.................................
Date of preparation.................................
Design team..
Latest date of revision.............................

**OPERATIONAL PLANNING
LOGICAL FRAMEWORK**

Narrative Summary	Verifiable Indicators	Methods of Verification	Risks and Assumptions
Strategic Objective: 1. **Goal:**	Impact on KRA	QQT Measures	
2. **Goal:**			
Outputs: 1.1 1.2 1.3 etc. 2.1 2.2 2.3 etc.	Performance indicators and service delivery targets	QQT Measures	
Activities: 1.1.1 1.1.2 etc.	Tasks/Inputs:	Cost £/$	
1.2.1 1.2.2 etc.			
1.3.1 1.3.2 etc.			
2.1.1 2.1.2 etc.	**TOTAL**	**£/$**	

Figure 11.1 _Template for a typical logframe_

QQT

A good and easy to remember acronym for tightening up your perform-ance indicators is QQT, which stands for quantity, quality, time. Don't just say you are going to train some people; say how many people, to what standard, and in what time frame. Try also to bear in mind that the indicators should, if possible, be objectively verifiable. You need to think about, and note in the matrix, what methods of verification will or could be used to measure progress, or to monitor and evaluate the outcome and impact of your efforts. In the example given it could be trainees qualifying in some way. It may be the actual commissioning of a new database when it is finally installed and the data are cleaned and verified. It could be the publication of a paper or feasibility report by a certain promised date.

Building the logframe with the team

The process of building the logframe matrix is best done through a series of workshops with the management team and ideally other stakeholders and partners. The following summary will provide a useful guide and aide-memoire to the purpose and the benefits of the workshop approach. I am grateful to Team Technologies Inc for the following synopsis of what they call the 'TeamUp Approach' (TeamUp is a registered trademark of Team Technologies Inc, USA). This method-ology for engaging stakeholders, as well as the principal users (the project team), in the process of building the logical framework has proved effective in hundreds of multi-million dollar technical assistance programmes and projects throughout the developing world and it is endorsed and used by most of the world's leading aid donors.

Workshop objectives for operational and action planning

■ To use a team-based approach to strengthen the design, imple-mentation and evaluation of an operating plan or change project.

■ To understand the purpose and requirements of effective project designs.

■ To introduce the logframe approach to project cycle management.

The benefits

This approach aims to strengthen project teams (and this for our purposes includes the business planning team) so that they are:

▌ informed;

▌ integrated;

▌ responsive;

▌ client-oriented;

▌ prepared for action; and

▌ productive.

The logframe:

▌ is a matrix tool for project cycle management (PCM) and for action planning;

▌ is vertically and horizontally integrated;

▌ works from the general to the particular;

▌ starts at the desired end result and works back to the present;

▌ links causes and effects and the external environment;

▌ facilitates performance measurement, reporting and evaluation.

Cause and effect – hierarchy of objectives

▌ Separate cause from effect, objectives from strategies, 'whats' from 'hows'.

▌ Use simple, concise statements for narrative summaries.

▌ Use strong action verbs.

Performance measurement – verifiable indicators

▌ If we can measure it we can manage it!

▌ Indicators must be targeted in terms of quantity, quality and time (QQT).

Monitoring, reporting and evaluation – means of verification

▌ Indicators and means of verification must be practical and cost-effective.

▌ Indicators and verification provide the basis for monitoring and evaluation systems and benchmarking.

External conditions – risks and assumptions

▌ Refine assumptions and perceived risks that are too general.

▌ Analyse their importance, probability and likely impact.

▌ Actively manage and influence assumptions during operational plan design and implementation.

▌ Plan for identified contingencies if possible. Avoid the foreseeable and minimize the impact of the unforeseen.

Logical framework strengths

▌ It meets the requirements of good project planning and action plan design.

▌ The design responds to past weaknesses.

▌ It is easy to learn and use.

▌ It reduces time and effort.

▌ It can be used internally for links to personal performance agreements and performance appraisal.

▌ It anticipates implementation.

▌ It sets up a framework for evaluation.

Logical framework limitations

▌ The logframe is not a substitute for other analyses, rather it is a synthesis of the products of these. Nor is it a substitute for a well-written and persuasive business plan. It can form an excellent appendix to such a document – particularly if a major change 'project' or programme is a significant feature of the business plan.

▌ Rigidity in project management may arise through overemphasis on the apparently linear nature of the hierarchy of objectives and lack of attention to systemic interdependencies.

▌ It cannot replace professional qualifications and experience in technical areas of operations and technical help should always be sought with the definition and scheduling of complex inputs.

▌ Its use requires a team process with good leadership and facilitation skills.

MANAGING PROJECT TEAM STRESSES

Two of the main causes of friction and disagreement, whether in project teams or normal business operations, are the failure to clarify individual, stakeholder and corporate expectations, and the failure to manage the issue of conflicting expectations when it arises. If employees are not either given directions – or better, afforded the opportunity to agree them – they will make up their own. Becoming attached to the comfort zone that such self-created horizons create, gives rise to automatic resistance to any attempts by management to propose alternative directions, exacerbated by people's natural fear of the unknown, as we saw in Chapter 9.

Apart from the central issue of the need to manage expectations and obvious complications surrounding time planning, prioritizing and even divided loyalties, there can be additional new stresses which are the result of employees being brought together in new teams or work groups where they may be unfamiliar with the methods, practices or even the culture of their new colleagues. Typically such project teams require a certain leadership style which has to be flexible if it is to adapt to the development of the team as it progresses towards greater productivity and higher performance. This competence which Ken Blanchard called 'situational leadership' was described in Chapter 8. Blanchard goes so far as to suggest that 'the most important function of a team leader is to help the group move through the stages of (team) development'.

Team building

These observations have been seen to be particularly relevant to project teams that are often thrown together for a specific period of time. They are often, in fact, under time pressure to produce measurable outputs (or 'deliverables' in project parlance), and yet frequently they are not accustomed to working together in close proximity or on the same task. Regardless of the make-up of the project team in terms of individuals' personality profiles, a newly created e-business unit or project team would probably do well to have some broad understanding of this behaviour pattern when embarking on their challenge. Furthermore, if such a group has a preponderance of bright young 'technocrats', senior management might well consider the wisdom posited by Meredith Belbin in his famous 1981 research on the ways in which different personality types tend to interact when they find themselves members of what may need to be an effective team. The technologically bright innovators or 'plants' as Belbin called them are unlikely to be effective or efficient at coordinating the results of the group's efforts, or sticking to a timetable, or selling their recommendations to others such as sceptical board members or shareholders. It would be rare for these attributes to feature significantly in their typical personality profile. Just as in everything else, balance is desirable to achieve the necessary effectiveness, and a certain deliberate 'social engineering' of the new venture team may be a wise move if collaboration, consensus and timely outputs are required.

Outcomes versus outputs; impact versus inputs

There is also a danger that project teams planning operational activities can easily get drawn into the minutiae of the organizational machinery and forget the all-important external perspective. This is because they get so caught up in the management of the project and most of them would feel that they do not have to think about the leadership. They cannot, however, afford an insular or inward-looking perspective. The customers, clients, society at large, and even to some extent partners such as suppliers and distributors, do not need to know all about your internal processes and mechanisms. They have no interest whatsoever in whether your appraisal system accurately reflects the necessary cascading of objectives and targets down to individual personal levels, or whether these individuals will need or receive training to be able to achieve them. They are only interested in the outcomes and not in your organizational or departmental outputs. One of the coaching responsibilities of leadership is constantly and gently to remind people of this, and stimulate them to check every planned input for its possible (and preferably measurable) contribution to the overall external impact of your performance improvement efforts. The next chapter highlights the ways to make sure that your performance management system captures both of these perspectives to deliver the extraordinary results that you need for continuous improvement, competitive advantage and excellent service delivery.

12

Empowering extraordinary performance

The nature of people is to strive ardently to reach a goal when they are committed. Put your people into a situation where their only choice is to commit to your goals and they will succeed beyond their limits.

Sun Tzu

INTERNAL AND EXTERNAL FOCUS

Covey (1992) provides what he calls a 'Universal mission statement'. It reads: 'To improve the economic well-being and quality of life of all stakeholders.'

He points out wisely that this should in no way replace your own organizational goals, but that it might possibly direct or guide their definition and provide context and coherence for everything else. There is a requirement here for a sense of stewardship. This is not just stewardship of a vision of where the organization wishes to be in the future (as we discussed earlier in the book). It is stewardship of the interests of all those – both inside and outside the business – who have an interest in the welfare (or the failure) of the organization on its journey towards that vision. It is not far removed from John Adair's original concept of the need to align and balance attention to the task, team maintenance and individual needs if, as I suggested earlier, we think of the 'team' as including all key stakeholders with an interest in improving performance.

The universal nature of this statement and the high-level principles that underpin it make it equally applicable to organizations in either the private or the public sector. This is essentially because it is outward looking and not self-serving. There is an assumption here – a certain knowledge – that if you look after customers and all other stakeholders, and strive to improve their economic well-being, you will ensure (and insure) that of the organization itself. Most mission statements have traditionally been geared to the interests of shareholders. Sadly the lust for golden eggs often results in the exploitation, ill health, or even the demise of the goose, which is yet another 'agricultural' metaphor to remind us that organizations, both public and private, are living systems that need to be nurtured if they are to perform optimally. It is sad enough for the individuals concerned when production companies are forced to lay off workers because of competition or market forces from parts of the global marketplace where labour costs are cheaper. It seems to me particularly tragic when the same thing happens to knowledge businesses where, usually as a result of takeovers, the most highly trained and talented people like designers or computer engineers are jettisoned to cut costs and preserve short-term profitability. In one recent case hundreds of high-grade knowledge workers were 'let go' while at the same time millions were spent on commissioning the design of the new corporate logo that would update the image and be appealing in every corner of the globe. What price Steven Covey's universal mission statement in such cases?

It is relatively easy to see that a high-level vision or mission statement can sit at the apex of a hierarchy of objectives. The pyramid of mechanisms and processes that are designed to achieve these cascade down first to address the relatively small number of key results areas and strategic objectives and finally the plethora of individual activities and inputs that are necessary for the mission's ultimate achievement. But the vast majority of these mechanisms and processes are essentially internal concerns, as we have seen. We should remember that justice has not only to be done: it has to be seen to be done. We need to find ways of linking the tools and methodologies and processes to things that matter to customers and other stakeholders, and articulate the ways in which successful performance can be evidenced to them in meaningful ways. This is exactly what the concept of Client Service Charters and the Chartermark programme in the UK managed to achieve, initially in the public sector but rapidly thereafter in the business world as well. The potential benefits of constantly raising the bar and forcing up standards for all stakeholders soon became apparent.

BENCHMARKING EXCELLENCE

In Chapters 7 and 8 we saw how a balanced scorecard can help the executive team to ensure that they maintain a similar balance between internal and external perspectives. The EFQM Excellence Model was illustrated as a user-friendly and practical tool to identify many AFIs across the board of operations and stakeholder interests. This was during the analytical stages of the strategic planning process to consider all aspects of activities and processes that can influence and frame strategies for improvement. It was also for the difficult job of identifying and balancing the vital few priorities that should be included in each annual operating plan.

The most popular and influential use of such tools, like the Malcolm Baldridge Quality Award System in the United States and particularly the EFQM Excellence Model in Europe, has been for benchmarking progress in continuous improvement. This benchmarking can be against a base-line score that is derived the first time the executive team conducts a self-assessment exercise (using the recommended and internationally accepted scoring systems), or from previous scores. It may also be against the published scores of known competitors or similar organizations, or with a view to externally validated accreditation for international awards or 'best-in-class' status. There is a wealth of good material in the public domain and available on the World Wide Web to assist business leaders who are interested in leading their executive management teams in the process of benchmarking or self-assessment for excellence. There are also a number of experienced consulting firms on both sides of the Atlantic that can facilitate the process and thus enable the leader or leaders themselves to be just another member of the team when it subjects itself to this rigorous scrutiny and corporate health check.

LINKING THE PLANS TO PERFORMANCE MEASUREMENT

I have pointed out that the operating plans themselves should ideally contain performance indicators and delivery targets that should obviously be measurable. Breaking down the work into bite-sized pieces for which individual managers and employees can be held accountable will clarify and help to manage expectations. Some employees may not be used to being put on the spot in this way and may be inclined to resistance or fear of this at first. Many, however, will soon come to prefer the fact that they know what is expected of them and that they will be given the chance to agree this. The corollary is often that they will be left to get on with it. They will be given results to achieve rather than jobs to do. The system is empowering if used properly. It is easy to see, therefore, how personal objectives and targets (and also those for teams) can be distilled from the overall plan and incorporated into individual performance agreements that can form part of the organization's performance review and appraisal system. Effective use of such an appraisal system completes the process of the performance management cycle from a purely internal corporate perspective. We need, however, to consider the ways to make such use fully effective from the perspective of people outside the organization who interact with it in its operating environment and who do not ever come into direct contact with these internal processes.

VALUE FOR MONEY

Ultimately I suggest that it can only be fully effective if we also have mechanisms for monitoring and evaluating the external perspective – what customers think, what partner organizations like suppliers and distributors think, and what the overall impact of our operations are on society in general. For these indicators we need to look to customer satisfaction surveys, questionnaires, focus groups, regular partnering meetings (and agreements), or client service charters with service delivery promises in plain language, effective mechanisms for feedback or complaints, redress, and the publication of benchmarked performance measures. In short, for every measure we use internally, we should seek to find an equivalent source of evidence that the measure is, in fact, valid in terms of what we really need to know. Is there a direct and demonstrable cause and effect linkage to the external perception of worth and value for money?

We need to be satisfied furthermore that people at all levels in the organization understand this dimension. If it is a public service organization do they really understand why their job exists and for whose benefit? Increasingly they do but to achieve the paradigm shift, where it is evident, has taken extraordinarily visionary leadership. This, in turn, has needed to be evidenced from top to bottom throughout organizations that have made the transition and the transformation to new ways of working and a new world-view. The new paradigm has, in fact, empowered people at all levels to discover, develop and use their latent leadership potential and skills. This, in turn, motivates and encourages others and a virtuous circle of continuous improvement, particularly in the right kinds of decision making, is the result. The organization, taking its lead from the leadership, learns how to be more effective as well as how to be more efficient. Extraordinary results are chalked up internally, and extraordinary benefits accrue to all stake-holders. Where this is seen to work well it is because leadership and not the performance management system is the primary source of influence. The latter can only ever be a tool to support effective leadership and management practices.

PERFORMANCE REVIEW AND APPRAISAL

The purpose of any performance management system, then, is to support and provide a framework for the leadership's role of encouraging the development of the required new paradigm that is to be one of high performance. Therefore we must find a good way of monitoring, evaluating and recording people's performance and somehow making this process developmental both for them and for the organization. The method normally used is the performance appraisal system. When people speak about performance management they normally think only of performance appraisal. For many years appraisal systems have tended to focus more on the process of performance (with attempts to rate behaviour or competence) than they have on results (which relate to personal objectives derived from those in corporate plans). More recently many systems have attempted to combine assessment of both dimensions and have usually failed in their job of helping to improve people's performance. Why do it if it is not going to be developmental, both for the individual and for the organization? When this happens the annual performance appraisal interview becomes a ritual, and a universally disliked one at that.

I do not intend to go into great detail about the pros and cons of the many forms of performance appraisal system, and I have specifically omitted discussion of the more sophisticated systems like 360 degree feedback. Once again there are numerous references available in the public domain and particularly on the World Wide Web for both commercial and public service organizations. Just try punching 'performance appraisal' into a search engine and look how many references you find! Suffice it to say that any appraisal system, even one that may be considered 'state of the art', will only ever be as good as the leadership's intention to take it seriously and require others throughout the organization to do likewise. Without such personal commitment and the intention to role model the required behaviour in promoting and using it, the appraisal system and the larger performance management system of which it is a part will collapse like a house of cards.

Many systems – or to be more accurate many appraisal documents or forms – include lists of descriptions of required competencies as well as the space to fill in agreed personal or team objectives. I will address the issue of competencies, particularly leadership competencies, in the next chapter. For now let us consider the problems of appraising people against objectives and whether or not we should attempt to do any more than this. Should we, for example, link performance ratings to remuneration or other rewards? Should we link them to promotion or recommendations for promotion? What about inadequate performance – should there be sanctions or pay cuts?

I think that the answers depend very much on the level of sophistication of the organization and its management, and particularly its HRM systems. A simple appraisal system that is understood and not feared by people at all levels will add value and contribute to individual and organizational development. This will be true even in the most highly developed of organizations, and most certainly in less sophisticated or less developed ones. An over-complicated, misunderstood, or threatening performance appraisal system will have absolutely the adverse effect and can be counterproductive, as a result of which it will quickly fall into disrepute with the danger that it will also undermine the rest of the overall performance management system. So the first message is: 'Keep it simple!' Bacal (1999) advocates this too and offers some useful comparisons between purely objective-based systems, those with ratings, and those with rankings. It is always difficult enough to try to link the process of defining, measuring and improving results to pay and other incentives. It is even more difficult to try to reward the associated process of defining, measuring and improving abilities and competence. Attempting to combine the two is stepping into a minefield and it is highly unlikely that you will come out unscathed. My advice is, don't do it!

What I would advocate is that if you are designing a new appraisal system, or having one designed, you should consider having it consist of three or possibly four parts. The parts that I suggest will not complicate it. On the contrary they will simplify it and make it more user-friendly in every way – something that most appraisal systems badly need!

Part 1. Preparation

It is obviously useful if both employees and their appraising manager give some time and thought to proper preparation for the review meeting or appraisal interview. I believe that this is one of those tasks that will tend undoubtedly to be put off by both parties if it is not structured. Consequently it is advantageous to have a document that constitutes Part 1 of the suite of performance appraisal forms and that captures the participants' preparatory thoughts and priorities. It should therefore provide sections that enable thoughts and suggestions about personal objectives, strengths and areas for improvement, training and development needs or desires, and future aspirations to be recorded from both parties' perspectives. It need not necessarily be retained as part of the formal suite of papers or electronic record if one is used.

Part 2. Performance agreement

The second part of the documentation should list objectives that are directly derived from those of the department or business unit and which should be SMART. Six is probably enough. There is no reason why some of them should not be team objectives to which the individual will be expected to contribute. The main point is that although these objectives may in many cases be drafted by the manager or appraising officer, they should be agreed by both parties, as should any targets or potential measures attached to them. This agreed list constitutes the main part of the performance agreement. It may even constitute a performance contract if this is appropriate. It may be appropriate in the case of the most senior managers to make them fully accountable, or in the case of any staff employed on a contract basis, for example for the duration of a project. In such cases the performance contract could probably form part of their legal contract of employment.

The performance agreement should also provide for agreement to be recorded concerning training and development needs and intentions. This not only helps to motivate employees and assure them that their personal development is important to the business, it provides for the cost of such agreement to be budgeted and scheduled, and helps to ensure that the whole review and appraisal process is seen as essentially developmental.

Part 3. The performance review

Part 3 of the documentation should provide for a review meeting at some intermediate point, usually six months on, during the appraisal period, which would normally be the operating year linked to the planning year. It gives both parties a chance to review whether the originally agreed objectives are still relevant and timely. If not they can be amended or new ones can be added. Whether or not any proposed training and development has taken place, and to what effect, can also be recorded. This provides an opportunity to monitor and evaluate not only whether the employee feels that they have personally benefited from such training and development, but whether the training was appropriate and cost-effective in the context of their enhanced competence and performance.

Part 4. The performance appraisal

At last we come to the part of the documentation that records the often dreaded appraisal interview itself. This appraisal is normally synonymous in most people's minds with the phrase 'performance management', but as I hope I have demonstrated, it is only one link in the chain, one piece of the systemic jigsaw. One benefit of limiting the appraisal to the discussion and judgement purely of objective achievement is that for most people it will be less threatening because it will be dealing with known quantities and therefore not likely to hold any nasty surprises. It will be literally *objective*. As soon as we introduce the issue of assessing competence, or marking people against competency descriptions (and thus judging their behaviour), we get into dangerous and potentially subjective territory.

Nevertheless, it is probably true that some individuals (particularly perhaps managers) could achieve apparently good and certainly required results by trampling all over their staff in an autocratic or tyrannical way and enforcing mute obedience through fear. I suggest that the results would be unlikely to be brilliant or significantly above expectations because people would not give of their best in such a situation. It is, however, a genuine cause for concern, particularly in cases where such managers may not themselves have a direct customer-facing role and where their lack of interpersonal skills could possibly remain undetected as long as the results of their subordinates were up to the mark. Particularly hard-driving sales managers of the old school come to mind. I have found this to be a danger in some developing countries where there tends to be a large power distance between 'bosses' and subordinates and where there may be little evidence of true leadership. Where authority is based purely on position or rank it can be dangerous to rely simply on achievement of objectives when appraising managers, but by the same token it would be equally dangerous to overcomplicate the system and introduce more subjectivity into what is probably already a discredited system. It is not easy.

In well-run organizations the answer is often seen to be the inclusion in the appraisal forms of a list of both generic and role-specific or specialist competencies against which people can be assessed. This affords the opportunity to include such things as interpersonal skills, coaching and mentoring skills, listening skills, negotiating skills, communications skills (oral and written) and so on. There are many lists of suitable generic management or supervisory competencies. What such lists do, however, is introduce very difficult questions about rating or scoring. How, for example, should you rationalize the score or rating from the overall competence assessment with that from the achievement of objectives or targets? Which is more important? Do they need weightings to reflect their relative importance?

If the leadership and the executive team can sort out these issues to their satisfaction, no doubt with advice from HR professionals or consultants, they may arrive at a happy compromise that suits the organizational purpose. If there is any doubt or insoluble argument around the subject, my advice would be to appraise performance purely in terms of the achievement of objective results. If the executive team wishes to include appropriate competencies and comment on them in the appraisal report (possibly in the context of identifying opportunities for training and development) these competency descriptions should be chosen from one of the professionally compiled lists or frameworks of standards and competencies. Wording behavioural descriptions is difficult. They should not be scored or rated. Furthermore, I would not advocate attempting to factor any assessment of overall competence in to the final assessment especially if this is in any way linked to pay.

Make this final assessment purely on actual performance for the majority of employees. Managers may be appraised on performance results that can include achievement of measurable targets for indicators of leadership competence. I will explain in Chapter 13 what I mean by this. If people at all levels are provided with opportunities to demonstrate their own leadership potential (which will often prove to be extraordinary), and encouraged to do so through being empowered to find innovative, adaptive, or generative ways to solve problems, they will achieve or exceed their agreed objectives anyway. They will also enjoy interacting with others to add value to this process so that the results become more than the sum of the parts.

Finally, do not ever forget that people can only give of their best if the support systems and appropriate organizational structures are in place. Remember that the organization or business is itself a complex and dynamic organism. The wheels need oiling occasionally and the mechanical parts need maintenance. People are not machines and nor are they drones. They need an enabling environment and a structure that offers the smallest possible number of impediments or barriers to extraordinary performance and to the development of leadership potential.

13

Developing the new extraordinary leadership competencies

The ultimate leader is one who is willing to develop people to the point that they eventually surpass him or her in knowledge and ability.

Fred A Manske Jr

DEFINITIONS

In the last chapter I introduced the idea of being able to appraise managers against indicators of leadership competence. Competence is one of those words that can describe a continuum – in this case a range of degrees of skill or ability. There can be varying degrees of competence on the way to being fully competent. In fact one could argue that in many, if not most, fields of endeavour there can be no such thing as being 'fully competent' because there is always room for improvement and our perceptions of competence change over time. The inexorable and fascinating process of athletes continuing to set new world records demonstrates this. Some definitions indicate that the word itself implies a *satisfactory level* of skill for the purpose intended. For example, if we described someone as a competent leader it could almost be interpreted as 'damning with faint praise'. Why not say a fully competent leader, an effective leader, an impressive leader, or an extraordinary leader unless you mean deliberately to qualify the description?

But this is semantics. Over the last 10 years or so a whole industry has grown up around the competency movement and most human resource professionals at least know what they mean by competence. In fact they tend to avoid the word in isolation, perhaps because of its traditional vagueness, and refer instead to competency, competencies and units and elements of competence. One thing that the movement and its insights have achieved, among others, is a breakthrough in dealing with the old and previously insoluble problem of measuring and evaluating training effectiveness. It has, in fact, proved possible to define and describe standards of competent behaviour (in a specific context), and then go on to identify verifiable indicators and provide examples of the sort of evidence that one would require to confirm achievement of the standard. As a result it has finally been possible to design vocational training with reasonable confidence that the real practical learning that it produces can be effectively applied on the job. This is as opposed simply to building a store of theoretical knowledge that some students will be able to regurgitate more readily than others in examinations. The theoretical knowledge is required, of course, as much as it ever was, but when it is taught and learnt in the wider context of its being necessary to underpin practice and experience, it is much more likely to be retained and utilized.

CASE STUDIES

The popularity and success of the Harvard Method for the use of case studies in business schools is testimony to this. It has radically improved the traditional 'chalk and talk' pedagogy of university education, as indeed it needed to for what used to be called an 'applied' as opposed to a 'pure' subject or field of knowledge. Good as case studies are for helping students relate theory to practice, however, they still tend to analyse and make recommendations concerning someone else's practice. I always feel that it is a bit like asking a group to build a bridge between two desks using post cards and paper clips. After the usual and often excruciating process of sorting themselves out, and checking to find out if there are any bridge engineers in the group, they will normally succeed after a fashion and have some fun in the process. The trouble is that, like aviation simulators, there is very little pain if the whole thing collapses in a heap (or crashes and burns). The price of failure is not high, and accordingly, neither is the level of serious attention or learning. Nobody ever has to walk across the bridge to see if it will serve its purpose. Real case studies that students bring with them and which require them to apply their (and perhaps their group's) learning to real management or leadership problems back at the workplace, or assignments that require them to find such issues that require adaptive solutions and work plans are, of course, much more valuable.

OUTDOOR DEVELOPMENT

During the 1980s there arose a fashion for management development using the great outdoors. Unfortunately it rather fell into disrepute when it became apparent that this was a potentially lucrative business that anyone with a few outdoor pursuits qualifications could set up, claiming to be able to be able to develop managers – or even leaders. I say unfortunately because I believe that training of this kind had a lot to offer managers, and particularly leaders. Where it was run by true management development professionals that used the outdoors and the outdoor pursuits experts purely as a vehicle to heighten the practical experience and challenges and make them safe, it was often very powerful. In such cases it would never happen that participants would be unacceptably frightened, pushed beyond their limits, embarrassed, or endangered. Meaningful discussions that related each different challenge, whether physical, intellectual, spatial, or systemic, would be held after each group task and facilitated by people who were knowledgeable and skilled at making the connections back to the workplace.

Where the business was hijacked by opportunists, who may have been competent sailors or rock climbers but who knew nothing at all about developing managers or leaders, it tended to put a lot of people off. Even some famous names jumped on the bandwagon and polished their egos by frightening many women managers with unreasonable physical challenges or endangering the health of unfit middle-aged male executives! This is never necessary. It quickly became apparent that this management or team 'development' was not cost-effective as anything other than a few days' break in the fresh air and a chance to push oneself in personal terms if this is what one enjoyed and wanted to do. Frequently the learning, if there was any, was not 'captured' back at the workplace and it was often difficult for people, even those who had enjoyed the experience, to relate it to their everyday work challenges. Some very unfortunate accidents and the cost of insurance premiums for potential liability finally resulted in the demise of the method for all but a handful of the original well-respected practitioners.

Let us go back to the simple and relatively safe example of the bridge building exercise. Let us assume that one of the outdoor development tasks was that the group should, in a tight time frame, build a bridge over a real river using planks, barrels, rope and a lot of initiative. There would be one big difference. You got wet if it didn't work! If it didn't work, it was probably more a question of lack of analysis, lack of proper planning, lack of time or resources, lack of coordination, or perhaps lack of leadership and direction of the process by some poor unfortunate who was placed 'in charge' or possibly 'elected' for this particular exercise. One thing would be certain: none of the group would forget the experience or find it boring as a learning vehicle. It would have combined the requirements of both theory and practical application. It would have encompassed the dimensions of thinking, feeling and doing and, most importantly, it would have needed the group to work as a team and to take responsibility for solving *their* problem with new and adaptive work inputs.

This is not rocket science; the military have been doing it for 50 years in selection board tests. I do not advocate that business or public sector organizations should emulate them in this although some do! I do think that proper and creative use of the outdoor environment may still provide interesting opportunities for leadership development, not least because well-designed tasks enable, and often require, geographically widespread systems thinking and prioritizing that can emulate the complexity of the business operating environment. Some will say quickly that computers can do all this nowadays. Until someone can show me a computerized task or case study that will get you wet if you fail, I remain unconvinced. Programming in electric shocks, as I am told the Russians once did with their jet fighter flight simulators, is not permitted or recommended!

COMPETITIVE ADVANTAGE

It has been suggested that in an increasingly competitive world, countries ultimately compete on the strength of their public sectors.

This is an interesting idea because public services worldwide are endeavouring to become more 'business-like', particularly in respect of their increased recognition of the need for customer focus and value for money. Furthermore, we can see from recent history that countries with public sectors that have totally failed to deliver economic growth and stability in fiscal and expenditure management policy (through being wedded to ideologies that simply did not work; through the scourge of corruption; or perhaps both) have indeed failed to be competitive. There has been no leadership worthy of the name. I am convinced that where, on the other hand, countries build really competitive economies, it is always a factor of a sustained history of leadership competence and integrity. This does not simply refer to the supreme office (such as the presidency of the United States, many of whose incumbents' personal values and principles have been questioned over the years). It refers to an overall climate and paradigm of essentially sound leadership at all levels.

Some will say that just as a geographical accident of birth can afford any individual a better or worse chance of material success or long life expectancy, so some unfortunate benighted countries (most of them in Africa or elsewhere in the Southern hemisphere), have never had a proper chance. When rationalizing like this, one can also easily blame colonial history, bureaucracy, the Cold War, corruption, climate, or even remoteness.

I will be controversial and say that I don't buy any of it; and I have visited, and lived and worked in, more 'third world' countries than most! All these factors present huge challenges but I believe that it all comes down to what Steven Covey calls 'principle-centred leadership' and what I have called 'extraordinary leadership'. The former has been notable for its absence in many poor and consequently less-developed countries and, until Nelson Mandela's return, in South Africa as well. The latter, if applied effectively from a firm foundation that is built on fundamental values and principles, will always attract support in the form of international aid (from the IMF, The World Bank and numerous other multilateral and bilateral donors). I am well aware of the arguments surrounding debt burden, and whether or not the influence and interventions of these agencies has been generally beneficial or harmful, and I do not intend to pursue them here.

Perhaps much more importantly from the standpoint of economic sustainability, good and principled leadership will attract foreign partnership for investment in the opportunities afforded by the often abundant natural resources, and this includes the people. Far from moving in to plunder the resources and exploit local workers, foreign investors will rightly give a wide berth to places with a history of instability and wholesale endemic corruption. I believe that Steven Covey would probably suggest that commercial businesses are essentially no different to public sectors, and that competitive advantage will ultimately be based on the integrity of the leadership and the values and competencies that leaders advance and role model for their organizations.

EMERGING TRENDS IN PUBLIC SECTOR LEADERSHIP DEVELOPMENT

If we can recognize and perhaps define 'good practice' in this way, it ought to be possible to distil its essence and to 'bottle it'. We need, however, to guard against confusing values and principles with the practice and competence that they must underpin. I believe that the private sector has much to learn from the public sector in this respect. Most commercial companies do not have the time or resources to develop comprehensive frameworks of good practice unless they are very large. When such large firms do develop good materials it is naturally in their competitive interests to keep the information to themselves rather than to share it selflessly with others as public services now do. The same applies to most consulting or management training firms, and even sadly to university business schools who also compete to sell their wares in a very fierce market for MBA students. The good news for all is that the Internet is now a valuable and regularly updated source of knowledge about international best practice.

The Australian public service has done a particularly good job of both the development and publication of materials as far as public sector requirements are concerned. A wealth of useful material is available on the World Wide Web at the Public Service Merit Protection Commission's (PSMPC) Web site at: http://www.psmpc.gov.au/leadership/.

The Management Charter Initiative (MCI) in the UK has developed comprehensive management standards, including senior management standards that also address the issues and competencies of leadership, with more of a private sector focus, although as I have pointed out elsewhere in this book, much of the material will be found to be generic and transferable with a little imagination. Their Web site can be found at: http://www.bbi.co.uk/mci.

The use of management standards for vocational qualifications has been developed further by MCI than in most other countries, as far as I am aware. The standards are set out with narrative behavioural descriptions and broken down into units and elements of competence. The required underpinning knowledge is detailed, as are suggestions for the sort of evidence that will be required when building a portfolio for independent assessment and qualification. The vocational qualifications are available at five levels, and although one should hasten to point out that they do not equate with academic qualifications, levels 3 to 5 are seen to be more or less practical alternatives to Certificate, Diploma in Management Studies, and MBA respectively. Sadly they do not yet have the kudos and therefore the popularity of the academic equivalents, especially the MBA. They do have the significant advantage that they facilitate work-based learning and require the compilation of portfolios of evidence for practical experience on the job. The personal development does not require the employee to be away for months or even years of study and it is not expensive.

The Canadian Government has launched a Leadership Network which also offers an impressive range of guides, documents and articles reflecting international best practice, and includes a lot of material on leadership competencies. This can be found at: http://www.leadership.gc.ca.

The Public Service Commission (PSC) of Canada, through their Personnel Psychology Centre, has also published *The Wholistic Competency Profile – A mode* (Slivinski and Miles, 1996–1997). This is a detailed guide and user's kit in four parts: Introduction, Building Competency Profiles, Assessing Competencies, and Human Resource Management Applications. The authors justify their spelling with a 'W' saying:

> *The primary reason we used the 'W' is because the model is about the whole person, the whole range of competencies and behavioural indicators, the whole organization, and the whole range of HRM applications. To call it Holistic Competency Profile: A Model seemed incongruous.*

The PSC in Canada has also commissioned some useful research into competency frameworks and tools and published the results. They may be found on the Web at their site: http://www.psc-cfp.gc.ca/research/personnel/comp_frame_e.htm. The purposes of the 1998 research by Sally Luce and Brian Lynch were:

▮ To provide context for creating and reviewing:

  – competency-based HR systems and subsystems

- competency tools and assessment

- competency policy and critical issues.

▌ To tease apart the vast competency literature.

▌ To develop an examination framework for competency concepts.

▌ To determine areas for further research and analysis:

- for practical information for operational decisions

- for support to policy and programme development.

The paper has the merit of being brief and of asking a lot of questions to stimulate thinking. It concludes with the following questions that all organizational leaders should perhaps consider: What do we expect from competency-based approaches, and are we prepared to do the work necessary to measure their impact? What will happen if we do not use competency-based approaches?

CHARACTERISTICS OF GOOD PRACTICE IN LEADERSHIP DEVELOPMENT

In Australia the PSMPC has conducted research with a wide range of agencies and has identified seven characteristics of good practice leadership development. They suggest that it:

1. recognizes that leadership is contextual, and is circumstance and culture specific;

2. focuses on meeting, and is structured around, key business object-ives and challenges;

3. acts as a vehicle for change;

4. puts responsibility for development on the individual;

5. forms part of an integrated system, using capability models and core programmes;

6. is driven by top management; and

7. makes use of a diverse range of resources, methodologies and approaches to learning, often using consortiums or partnerships.

In recognition of the importance of these characteristics, the PSMPC has developed a Senior Executive Leadership Capability Framework. This has five component core criteria for high performance by senior executives and embodies essential values including, and in particular, that leadership of the highest quality is essential to the achievement of high performance within an environment of change.

LEADERSHIP CAPABILITY FRAMEWORKS

The principal role of senior executive leaders in any business or organization is to play a key part in continuously improving the whole process of delivery of the core service functions of the business to customers and stakeholders. In Chapter 7 we explored how this necessitated far more than dreaming up a vision or strategies for its achievement. They also need to frame policy and strategy and get personally involved to coach others through the difficulties of solving the day-to-day problems of new adaptive and generative work.

In this context they have a particular accountability to ensure the delivery of outputs that contribute to the achievement of outcomes as determined by these customers and stakeholders, as we saw in Chapter 11. They must be able to take the overview and focus on the linkages between the different and sometimes conflicting sets of output priorities. This requires them to create a shared vision and sense of purpose for their organization, and to enable and motivate their staff to achieve high performance.

Any capability or competencies framework seeks to capture and establish a shared understanding of the critical success factors for performance in a role – in this case the leadership role. In Chapter 1 I discussed the basis of leadership competence and in Chapter 3 I listed some competencies for extraordinary leadership influence that had been mentioned piecemeal in the course of these first three chapters. This list, or better still your own list, can form a subset for any of the published and normally well-researched lists like that adopted by the Australian Public Service. A full description of their framework can be

found on the Web at: http://www.psmpc.gov.au/leadership/
supplement.htm.

A good framework will be potentially useful for a number of
applications that could include:

▌ selection;

▌ leadership development;

▌ performance management;

▌ short- and long-term succession planning;

▌ broader organizational development initiatives.

Application of a framework (with flexibility as the watchword) in a
coherent way, and as a policy and strategy tool for the whole systemic
range of leadership-related endeavours, will contribute to the achievement and sustainability of a culture of high-quality leadership in any
organization. It is, in fact, the consistency and coherence of application
across the board (or across the balanced scorecard) that would make
the results extraordinary. The competencies are not extraordinary in
themselves and it matters not whether we borrow others' definitions
or invent our own list. There is enough agreement about perceptions
of best practice to make these essentially generic. My point is that
extraordinary high performance (by individual leaders, or by their staff,
or by their organization as a whole) will result from the adoption of a
policy and strategies to incorporate development of these competencies
intravenously into the whole organizational living system. To revert to
the gardening metaphor that I used earlier, the application of systemic
fertilizers and the right sort of caring is as important, if not more
important than the use of new machinery or tools.

Behaviours and indicators

One of the most difficult things to do when attempting to create a
competency or, as the Australians call it, a capability framework, is to
agree the best form of words for descriptions of the standards of
behaviour on the one hand, and the indicators by which we can judge

or assess people against these, on the other. If you try this you will find that there is a tendency for descriptions of suitable indicators to be almost the same as those of the standards or capabilities. I have to say that my one criticism of the otherwise admirable PSMPC Senior Executive Leadership Capability Framework is that it tends to fall into this trap. The indicators are often really just an expanded and more detailed description of behaviour and not quantifiable or even truly qualitative measures for the degree of competence achievement.

I admit that the more strategic the competencies we are attempting to describe, the more difficult it becomes to pin down and qualify verifiable indicators. Just as we found that it is possible when framing objectives and outputs during the strategic planning process to make them SMART and to qualify the performance indicators by means of QQT, we must attempt to do the same with indicators for assessment of competence, even though we think we know it when we see it!

Once more, let me introduce a caveat here, however. I advocated the use of the Excellence Model principally as a strategy development tool and said that its more popular use for assessment, scoring and benchmarking was for many organizations (at least initially) secondary. I think that the same can apply to the use of competency or capability frameworks, whether for leadership or any other workplace standards. Even the recognition that a desirable or perhaps increasingly required set of competencies will be used to underpin and coordinate the personal development, performance management and succession planning systems, and encouragement of understanding of how this can structure or guide the route to high performance, will have a significant impact in any organization. There is no need to attempt to go the vocational qualifications route and get bogged down in attempts to pin down evidential requirements for every element of competence. Analysis is not strategy and not a means to put strategy into action.

MULTIPLE INTELLIGENCES

We have seen how certain extraordinary and often resilient types of individual have sometimes come to the fore and proved to have the right leadership capabilities for the time and place in which they found themselves. We have seen how the nature of what we now see as being necessary for 21st-century organizational leadership effectiveness is somewhat different in style from the model accepted and perhaps advocated by previous generations. Nevertheless, it is likely that personal qualities that are seen as 'admirable' are those which have always been seen as such, because they reflect fundamental ethical values. As Mant (1999) says in the introduction to his book, 'Like the geographical features seen on a journey, the fact that they hardly change doesn't reduce the pleasure of seeing them afresh.'

We have seen how the model for this mix of competencies is unfortunately not 'ordinary' in that 'ordinary management' does not require such a comprehensive and uncommon set of skills, or 'multiple intelligences' as Alistair Mant prefers to call them. He lists seven basic elements which taken together add up to the cause of successful leadership. Indeed he arranges them in causal sequence to show how each element plays a part in causing the others. They are as follows:

1. Authority.

2. Purpose.

3. Judgement.

4. Systems ('frog') thinking.

5. Sanity.

6. Broad-based intelligence.

7. The virtuous circle – which should enable new generations of purposeful and resourceful leaders to emerge quite naturally.

Given the unprecedented demands that maintaining competitiveness or competitive advantage places on corporate or organizational leaders in the light of the new global economy, perhaps what may be 'extraordinary' may nevertheless have to become more commonplace, as I have implied elsewhere. It should be capable of being identified at an early stage (of managers' or potential leaders' careers), and capable of being encouraged and developed. It may also be true to say that it may need to be held in higher regard. Its extraordinary rarity should perhaps give it a premium value that results in more serious and continuous efforts to identify and nurture it. It should be prized rather than perceived as eccentric, non-conformist or plain threatening, as has often been the case in conservative hierarchical (and one has to say

male-dominated and often large) organizations that routinely demonstrate wholesale neglect or absence of the above intelligences or
competencies.

CHARTING STRATEGIC DILEMMAS

Hampden-Turner (1990) suggests that a key required competency for
leaders is the ability to confront strategic dilemmas. This seems to make
a lot of sense and supports the logic of recognizing some of the dilemmas
that I have identified in this book, such as the central requirement to
manage both performance and uncertainty at the same time. He
presents a variety of tools for helping management teams to do this
creatively and he summarizes the process in seven steps:

1. *Eliciting the dilemmas.* Identifying the opposed values that form the
   'horns' of the dilemma, for example cost as opposed to quality, or
   local initiative as opposed to central coordination and control.
   Hampden-Turner suggests that humour can be a distinct asset in
   this process since 'the admission that dilemmas even exist tends
   to be difficult for some companies'.

2. *Mapping.* Locating the opposing values as two axes and helping
   managers identify where they see themselves, or their organization,
   along the axes.

3. *Processing.* Getting rid of nouns to describe the axes of the dilemma.
   Present participles formed by adding 'ing' convert rigid nouns into
   processes that imply movement. For example, central control versus
   local control becomes 'strengthening national office' and 'growing
   local initiatives'. This loosens the bond of implied opposition
   between the two values. It becomes possible to think of 'strengthening national services from which local branches can benefit', or
   building central technological know-how and capacity for e-sales
   with which existing sales channels can establish 'hot links'.

4. *Framing contextualizing.* Further softening the adversarial structure
   among different values by letting 'each side in turn be the frame
   or context for the other'. This shifting of the 'figure-ground'
   relationship undermines any implicit attempts to hold one value

as intrinsically superior to the other, and thereby to become mentally closed to creative strategies for continuous improvement of both.

5. *Sequencing.* Breaking the hold of static thinking. Very often, values like low cost and high quality appear to be in opposition because we think in terms of a point in time, not in terms of an ongoing process. For example, a strategy of investing in new process technology and developing a new production-floor culture of worker responsibility may take time and money in the near term, yet reap significant long-term financial rewards.

6. *Waving/cycling.* Sometimes the strategic path towards improving both values involves cycles where both will get 'worse' for a time. Yet, at a deeper level, learning is occurring that will cause the next cycle to be at a higher plateau for both values.

7. *Synergizing.* Achieving synergy where significant improvement is occurring along all axes of all relevant dilemmas (this is the ultimate goal, of course). Synergy, as Hampden-Turner points out, is a uniquely systemic notion, coming from the Greek *syn-ergo* or 'work together'.

This seven-step process should be very useful for management teams (and leaders in particular) who find themselves on the horns of a dilemma – or perhaps several – in the context of trying to work out a viable e-strategy.

ATTRACTING AND RETAINING THE BEST

The issue of retention, or 'internal recruitment' as the Armed Forces used to call it, is now more important than ever. It costs a lot of money to select, recruit, train and develop new generations of leaders and you don't want to lose them to competitors who will be ever ready to poach them once you have a reputation for 'growing' them. It is interesting to look at how some leading e-business companies are rising to the challenges of attracting and retaining the brightest and the best. Huge and seductive attractions now await graduates with the right perceived qualities. Five-star working conditions, smart cars and 'golden handcuffs' were the norm in Silicon Valley until the dramatic drop in the stock values of (what were always overvalued) dotcom companies in the markets in early 2001, and they will be again as things settle down and sense prevails. The correction was necessary and a timely reminder of much of what I have said about the need for sound planning strategy, and above all sound leadership, to be no different for hi-tech or Internet-based ventures.

But when we see these attraction and retention incentives are we talking about extraordinary technological ability, extraordinary entrepreneurial insight, or extraordinary potential leadership? Will the qualities perceived as being necessary for the latter, some of which I have outlined and discussed in this book, still be relevant and appropriate in 10 years' time? It has been the central message of the book to suggest that they probably will – extraordinary though they may be.

References

Bacal, R (1999) *Handbook of Performance Management*, A Briefcase Book, McGraw-Hill, Maidenhead

Bennis, W (1984) *An Invented Life: Reflections on leadership and change*, Addison-Wesley

Bennis, W and O'Toole, J (2000) 'Don't hire the wrong CEO', *Harvard Business Review*, May–June

Binney, G and Williams, C (1997) *Leaning into the Future – Changing the way people change organizations*, Nicholas Brealey, London

Bratt, S and Gallacher, H (1988) *The Facilitators Support Kit*, BQC Ltd, http://www.bqc-network.com

Carnall, C A (1995) *Managing Change in Organizations*, Routledge, London

Covey, S (1992) *Principle-Centred Leadership*, Franklin Covey Co, Simon & Schuster, New York

Dixon, N (1979) *On the Psychology of Military Incompetence*, Futura, London

Drucker, P – quote in second para of section on 'Analysis, planning and action' – has no reference

Gates, W (1999) *Business @ the Speed of Thought*, Warner Books

Guirdham, M (1995) *Interpersonal Skills at Work*, Prentice Hall Europe, Hemel Hempstead

Haines, S with McCoy, K (1995) *Sustaining High Performance: The strategic transformation to a customer-focused learning organization,* St Lucie Press

Hampden-Turner, C (1990) *Charting the Corporate Mind,* The Free Press, New York

Heifetz, R and Laurie, D (1997) 'The work of leadership', *Harvard Business Review,* January–February (based in part on Heifetz's book, *Leadership Without Easy Answers,* Belknap Press of Harvard University Press)

Kaplan R S and Norton D P (1992) *Harvard Business Review,* January

Kotter, J (1999) *Leading Change,* Harvard University Business School Press

Mant, A (1997) *Intelligent Leadership,* Allen & Unwin, Sydney

Mintzberg, H (1994) *The Rise and Fall of Strategic Planning,* Prentice Hall, New York

Modahl, M (2000) *Now or Never – How companies must change today to win the battle for the Internet customer,* Orion Business Books and HarperCollins, New York

Peters, T and Waterman, R H (1988) *In Search of Excellence,* Warner Books

Senge, P (1990) 'The leader's new work: building learning organizations', *The Sloan Management Review,* Fall

Senge, P (1990) *The Fifth Discipline: The art and practice of the learning organisation,* Doubleday/Currency, New York

Senge, P (1990) The leader's new work, *Sloan Management Review,* 15, Fall

Slivinski, L W and Miles, J (1996–1997) *The Wholistic Competency Profile – A Mode'* The Public Service Commission of Canada, published on the Internet by the Personnel Psychology Centre of the PSC: www.psc-cpf.gc.ca, see also: www.leadership.gc.ca

Stacey, R (1996) *Strategic Management & Organizational Dynamics,* Pitman, London

Sun Tzu (1995)'The Art of War', in Donald G Krause, *The Art of War for Executives,* Berkely Publishing Group

Taffinder, P (1995) *The New Leaders,* Kogan Page, London

Zalesnik, A (1977) 'Managers and leaders – are they different?', *Harvard Business Review,* May/June

Zalesnik, A (1989) *The Managerial Mystique,* Harper & Row, New York

Index